where,   don't know when,   But I   know we'll meet a - gain some sun - ny

day. _____   Keep   smil - in' thro'   just like

you   al - ways   do   Till the   blue skies drive the   dark clouds far a -

way. _____   So will   you   please say hel - lo _____ to the   folks that I know, _ Tell them

3

WE'LL MEET AGAIN

WE'LL MEET AGAIN

VERA LYNN

With Robin Cross and Jenny de Gex

SIDGWICK & JACKSON
London

First published in Great Britain in August 1989 by Sidgwick & Jackson Limited
First reprint September 1989
Second reprint October 1989
Third reprint November 1989

ISBN 0-283-99868-7

Typeset by Rowland Phototypesetting Limited
Bury St Edmunds, Suffolk
Printed in Great Britain by
The Bath Press Limited, Bath
for Sidgwick & Jackson Limited
1 Tavistock Chambers, Bloomsbury Way
London WC1A 2SG

CONTENTS

1

SHADOWS OF WAR

On 29 September 1938 I was singing with the Ambrose band at the Hammersmith Palais in London. That day Neville Chamberlain, the British Prime Minister, was keeping a date of a very different kind, at Munich with Adolf Hitler. War was in the air. At home in Britain over 30 million gas masks had been issued to men, women and children; trenches were being dug in our public parks to serve as air-raid shelters; barrage balloons billowed into the sky over London; plans for the mass evacuation of the civilian population were laid.

On the 30th Neville Chamberlain returned from Germany clutching the famous scrap of paper which bore Hitler's signature and assuring the crowds in Downing Street that he had secured 'Peace for our time.' The spectre of war seemed, for the moment, to recede. But we had been granted only a temporary reprieve. The trappings of war had been let out of the box and could not be put away. The gas masks, air-raid precautions (ARP), blackout preparations, and fear of air attack itself became increasingly familiar features of life as the conflict drew near. Meanwhile we re-armed. We built the Hurricanes and Spitfires which were to save us in the Battle of Britain. Thousands of men joined the Territorial Army. By the summer of 1939 the Civil Defence services had enrolled over a million new recruits.

Vera Lynn pictured with Ambrose's Octet in the late 1930s. It was while touring with the Ambrose Orchestra in the autumn of 1939 that she first sang 'We'll Meet Again'.

Neville Chamberlain on his return from the Munich Conference in September 1938. In his hand is the piece of paper bearing Hitler's worthless promise to renounce all warlike intentions against Britain. That night excited crowds in Downing Street greeted Chamberlain with 'For He's a Jolly Good Fellow', but there was to be no 'peace for our time'.

I was already aware of the suffering inflicted by the Nazis. In the summer of 1938 I joined an all-star cast at the Gaumont State Cinema, Kilburn, in a charity show supporting Eddie Cantor's appeal on behalf of Jewish refugees from Germany and Austria. The performers included Eddie Cantor himself, Gracie Fields, Max Miller, George Formby, Flanagan and Allen, Bea Lillie and Douglas Byng. Within two years we would be channelling our performing talents into the war effort.

Even after war broke out there was a lingering, and very British, feeling that the Nazis were faintly ridiculous figures. On Ambrose's provincial tour of 1939 band members Les Carew and Max Bacon had audiences in stitches with their impersonations of Hitler and Goering in a parody of 'Three Little Fishes' – Syd Colin completed the trio, playing Stalin. It was on this tour that I first sang 'We'll Meet Again'. Another number I introduced was 'You Can't Black Out the Moon'. A journalist who covered the tour wrote, 'I would like to prophesy a future for both of these tunes.'

Well, the blackout stayed with us for six years of war, and the words of 'We'll Meet Again' seem as apt to me today as when I first sang them:

We'll meet again, don't know where, don't know when,
But I know we'll meet again some sunny day,
Keep smiling through just like you always do
Till the blue skies drive the dark clouds far away.

The drift to war can be traced in the pages of the *East Ham Echo*, the local paper in Barking, where Vera Lynn lived in 1939.

On the surface all seems well. In January 1939 advertisements for an ambitious suburban development, Elm Park Garden City, were offering the 'Arcadia' home, with its 'sunny kitchen and double-size lounge, three bedrooms and tiled bathroom', for a down payment of £1 and weekly payments of 13s 6d, the solution to the housing problems of 'the £3 15s–£4-a-week man'.

H. Woodmansee and Sons, outfitters of Barking Road, were telling their customers that '1939 is going to be one of the best years for Smart New Designs, SO BE THE FIRST' to buy men's made-to-measure overcoats from 27s 7d to 43s 4d and suits from 35s to 70s.

Every week there were the usual local stories of assaults and affrays, usually outside public houses, car accidents and suicides, in most of which stalwart police sergeants in the 'Dixon of Dock Green' mould seemed to play a prominent role. In March those with deep pockets and a determination to cut a social dash might have been tempted by an advertisement placed by Jays, an electrical goods emporium, offering the His Master's Voice All-Wave Radio and Television Receiver, at 29 guineas or 6s a week on the never-never. Anyone who acquired a set would not have much time to enjoy the new service, which was closed down on 1 September, two days before the outbreak of war.

The *Echo*'s readers were regularly told the moral tale of advertisement anti-heroine 'Mrs Overtime' who, poor ignorant soul, uses soap suds alone and exhausts herself with frenzied rubbing and scrubbing. In contrast 'Mrs Sparetime' adds Mazo 'to energise her soap, and it does the work for her!'

In May the *Echo* introduced a woman's page, and on the 19th provided some 'Hints for Summer Brides – the bride of 1939 is particularly lucky, for there is a greater range of styles to choose from than ever'.

One does not have to look far to find more significant items. On

6 January the *Echo* carried a report about thirty Jewish refugee children who were to be accommodated by the Jewish community in East Ham. At the end of the month it covered the outbreak of a row which was to rumble on until September. East Ham's Air Raid Precautions (ARP) volunteers were up in arms against the local council over the delay and confusion which were hampering their effectiveness.

Air Raid Precautions had begun life in 1924 as a Home Office subcommittee under the chairmanship of Sir John Anderson. It sprang from the British civilian experience of bombing in the First World War, during which Germany had mounted 103 raids (fifty-one by airships), mostly on London. A total of 300 tons of bombs had killed 1413 people. The worst single bombing incident of the war occurred in London on 28 January 1918 when a 660 lb bomb hit the Odhams print works in Long Acre, killing thirty-eight and injuring eighty-five.

Although the raids had no influence on the course of the war, their psychological effect lingered on long after 1918. In the 1930s a new generation of bombers cast a long shadow over Europe. Many military thinkers believed that in any major conflict of the future vast fleets of bombers, pounding the enemy's capital to rubble, would decide the issue in a matter of hours. In 1932 Stanley Baldwin, then a prominent member of the coalition government, gloomily told the House of Commons, 'I think it is well for the man in the street to realize that there is no power on

Grim preparations for war. Workmen dig trench shelters on the quiet lawns of Lincoln's Inn Fields in London.

9

earth that can protect him from being bombed. Whatever people may tell him, the bomber will always get through. The only defence is in offence, which means that you have to kill more women and children more quickly than the enemy if you want to save yourself.' At Munich six years later Adolf Hitler played on Neville Chamberlain's fears by ominously observing that he too was a humanitarian and hated 'the thought of little babies being killed by gas bombs'.

In March 1935 Hitler proclaimed the existence of a new German air force, the Luftwaffe, boasting that it was already equal in size to the RAF. It was subsequently combat-tested during the Spanish Civil War, in which the destruction of the Basque town of Guernica by the bombers of the German Condor Legion provided a chilling image of the horrors of modern warfare. In the late 1930s British air planners anticipated that, if war came, the Luftwaffe might launch an overwhelming air attack on London, frequently referred to as the 'knock-out blow'. It would be as swift, sudden and shocking as the terrifyingly staged air raid in Alexander Korda's film version of H. G. Wells's *Things to Come*, a nightmare vision of mass panic and toppling landmarks. Extrapolating from the destruction caused by bombing in the Spanish Civil War, particularly the raids by Italian aircraft on Barcelona, the Air Staff calculated that the Luftwaffe could deliver 700 tons of bombs a day on London, with a possible 3500 tons in the first twenty-four hours, each ton causing at least fifty casualties. Their heads filled with these doom-laden figures, the Home Office calculated that in the first three months of such a war 60,000,000 square feet of coffin timber would be required to bury the dead. Revised costings resulted in the stockpiling of tens of thousands of collapsible papier-mâché and cardboard coffins.

Advised by leading experts, the government also planned for the psychological as well as the physical worst. The Ministry of Health joined the numbers game, estimating that it might have to deal with up to 4,000,000 mental cases in the first six months of war. In these circumstances it was assumed in government circles that civilian morale would crack almost instantly under air bombardment. Panic-stricken hordes of Londoners would pour out of the shattered capital into the countryside, where the government had laid contingency plans to turn them back, with machine-gun fire if necessary.

Experience during the General Strike of 1926 had demonstrated what might happen when Britain's principal channels of communication and distribution were paralysed. Power would have to be devolved to the regions, and in the 1930s twelve autonomous Civil Defence regions were established, with London counting as a single region. The chain of command ran down from the regional headquarters through the group headquarters to the borough. The borough HQ was often in the town hall, integrating the civil defence system with local government. In most towns council staff shared civil defence responsibilities with the small number of full-time civil defence personnel and the many local volunteers. Below the borough lay the district and then, at the bottom of the pyramid, the air-raid wardens' posts.

In theory each post, heavily sandbagged and clearly marked, was supposed to control an area containing approximately 500 people. In London there were about ten posts per square mile. In the Blitz the warden was to be the eyes and ears of the local Civil Defence Control Centre, patrolling the streets and controlling 'incidents', the bureaucratic euphemism invented to describe every sort of disaster inflicted on the civilian population by an air raid. It was the warden's report of an 'incident' that set the civil defence machine in motion, summoning stretcher parties, fire engines, heavy rescue units and mobile canteens – all the services required to care for the injured, comfort the survivors and dispose of the dead.

There were 1,500,000 civil defence personnel in 1939, over two thirds of them volunteers. Even at the height of the Blitz only 16,000 of London's 200,000 wardens were full-time, paid at the lowly rate of £3 a week. Initially, the air-raid warden was not a popular figure. The public's attitude towards him ranged from mild amusement at his flimsy blue overalls and tin helmet to the active hostility Britons tend to reserve for all those they see as interfering minions of the state. Before the bombs started to fall the warden was often regarded as a self-appointed (and possibly army-dodging) Peeping Tom, peering through people's blackout curtains; or as a strutting local gauleiter, harassing citizens about the buckets of water and sand in their offices – the model for the overbearing warden played by Bill Pertwee in 'Dad's Army'.

The integration of the civil defence system with that of local government meant that each borough's ARP was only as efficient as the authority itself, a factor which would cause many problems in the Blitz. Moreover, in working-class areas it was hard to attract volunteers. In February 1939 there were 615 volunteers in East Ham, against a wartime ARP establishment of 1643. Charges and countercharges flew back and forth in the correspondence columns of the *Echo*, and on 17 March the controversy entered a new phase when a 6d rise in the rates was in large part blamed on the estimated £47,000 ARP expenditure for the coming year, which included the cost of a bomb-proof headquarters built beneath the new technical college opposite the Town Hall. Two weeks later the council appealed to the householders of East Ham to help in their own defence, and also to relieve the cost of the rates, by erecting their own Anderson shelters when they were delivered.

On the night of 30 September 1917 some 300,000 Londoners had taken shelter in the capital's underground system during a German air raid. The government feared a repetition of these grim scenes in any future war and the development of a 'deep shelter mentality' by thousands of citizens, who would disappear underground and refuse to come to the surface. One countermeasure was to ensure the widest possible dispersion of civilians during a raid by distributing shelters which could be erected in householders' gardens.

The Anderson shelter was originally named after its designer, Dr David A. Anderson, not the Home Secretary, Sir John Anderson, who announced the scheme in the autumn of 1938. Nevertheless, it is with the politician rather than the designer that the shelter is always associated. Consisting of fourteen sheets of corrugated iron, the shelter formed a shell 6 feet high, 4½ feet wide and 6½ feet long. It was buried to a depth of 4 feet and then covered with at least 15 inches of soil. It could accommodate up to six people in conditions of dank discomfort and was liable to frequent flooding. In the Blitz some people spent more time bailing or pumping out their Andersons than sheltering in them.

The Anderson shelter was issued free to all earning less than £250 a year and at a charge of £7 for those with higher incomes. Eventually 2,250,000 were erected and, in British fashion, made homely with bunks inside and flowers and vegetables planted in the protective bank of earth. After the end of the Blitz, in the summer of 1941, an American journalist wrote that 'there was a greater danger of being hit by a vegetable marrow falling off the roof of an air-raid shelter than of being struck by a bomb'.

The warden's post, heavily sandbagged and clearly marked, the lynchpin of the Civil Defence system. Early in 1940 the ARP and AFS (Auxiliary Fire Service) Magazine published the following ditty:
UNDER MY HELMET
Big-helmet Wilkie they call me,
Big-helmet Wilkie, that's me:
Now that they've made me a warden
I get my torch batt'ries free!

Once, at the sound of a warning.
A blonde cried, 'Shelter me please!'
Then said, 'That isn't a rattle;
Blimey – it's your knocking knees!'

Big-helmet Wilkie they call me,
Wilkie the Warden, that's me!

The arrival of the Anderson shelters in a London street. The shelter was issued free to all those earning less than £250 a year and at a charge of £7 for those on a higher income.

Only those with gardens in which to erect them – about 27 per cent of the population – benefited from the provision of the Anderson shelter. Everyone had been issued with a gas mask by the time of the Munich crisis in September 1938. For many people the sensation of clammy breathlessness and smell of rubber and disinfectant they experienced when donning the mask was the first intimation of the approaching war; the distribution of the masks by thousands of volunteers was their introduction to the communal effort which was to characterize the Home Front during the war years.

The fear of gas attack was very real. Thousands of crippled ex-servicemen were living reminders of the horrors of the gas attacks on the Western Front during the First World War; gas had been used by the Italians in their invasion of Ethiopia in 1935. ARP volunteers were drilled in anti-gas measures, gingerly sniffing tiny phials of the poisonous stuff to learn how to distinguish the distinctive odours of each type. In February 1938 the *Daily Express* reported:

Great doings in Paddington last night. Mythical enemy bombers wrecked houses, ripped (in theory) fifteen foot craters in the road and sprayed the Borough with mustard gas. It was the first air-raid demonstration conducted by a Borough Council in London and was designed to test the Air Raid Precautions service. Girls who had been 'burned' by mustard gas were rushed to the first-aid station in Paddington Central Baths. The first thing to do in such a case is to remove contaminated clothing. Two hundred people in the gallery saw nurses deprive the girls of their clothes. The organizers had previously warned 'casualties' to wear bathing costumes underneath. Paddington had been divided into twelve areas for Air Raid Precautions work. In last night's scheme only six areas took part. Home Office inspectors commented – 'Not bad for a first effort.'

Most children took quite happily to the special 'Mickey Mouse' gas masks designed to give this macabre precaution the appearance of a game. A 'gas helmet' was issued for babies, a small airtight chamber into which filtered air was pumped by means of a hand bellows. Mr E. W. Mills, a nurseryman of Hextable, Kent, invented a gas-proof perambulator, approved by the local ARP. It was built of wood with a triplex glass window, air valve, a filter from a gas mask and a large bulb at the rear to pump out the air – 'when the bulb is pressed, air is forced out via the valve, and the air is let in via the filter.'

On 17 March 1939, two days after Hitler had installed himself in the Hradcany Palace in Prague, the capital of the now dismembered Czechoslovakia, the *East Ham Echo* reported an inquest held at Stratford. A sixty-four-year-old former dining-room keeper, Charles Poliane, had committed suicide because of 'ill health . . . and his concern about national affairs and the possibility of another war.'

In Britain, public opinion hardened. Hitler was seen clearly as an aggressor. The next time he moved, he must be resisted. And now, with grim inevitability, the Führer's attention was shifting north, to Poland.

A nightmarish vision of the future. Post Office workers take part in an anti-gas exercise in 1937. During the crisis over Czechoslovakia in September 1938, 38 million gas masks were issued to men, women and children in Britain. The crisis induced symptoms of panic which included a spate of hasty marriages, a boom in the sale of wills and rumours that many people were beginning to hoard sugar and petrol.

Above: In the late 1930s, fear of poison gas attacks cast a long shadow. A baby disappears inside his gas helmet. Babies always emerged red as beetroots from the clammy confines of the helmet. *Below:* An experimental anti-gas train on the LMS Railway.

Above: Two models gamely don gas masks at a public health exhibition to demonstrate the facilities offered by an anti-gas service van. *Opposite, top:* Day trippers dressed for summer suddenly find themselves dressed for war during Chatham Navy Week. *Opposite, bottom:* A nun prepares for the worst. At least one of her colleagues is not amused by the performance for the cameras. For most people, the disagreeable experience of trying on a gas mask for the first time brought home the reality of approaching war.

In May every householder in East Ham received a pamphlet providing details of the evacuation scheme for the London area. That month there was a National Service exhibition at East Ham Town Hall. On opening day an army light tank and a trailer fire pump were put on display outside. At the entrance to the main hall there was a revolving dais with a 'lifelike' figure of Britannia, surrounded by models in the uniforms of the Army, Navy and Air Force, the fire services, the Police War Reserve and The Red Cross Nursing Service. It was a very English affair, indicative of the resignation with which most people now faced the inevitability of war. In a speech at the opening ceremony the MP for East Ham South, Mr A. Barnes, observed that, 'what we are engaged upon this afternoon is a very regrettable necessity, arising not from the actions or motives of our own people, but springing from circumstances over which they have no control. The purpose and function of this exhibition are to bring home to citizens that, should its people again be involved in warfare, they cannot look upon that incident as something that will be fought apart from their own shores. Every man, woman and child will be affected, in the military as well as the national sense.' Following him, Commander O. Locker Lampson MP warned the audience that if war should come, it might be a matter not of hours but of minutes before 'death comes to our doorsteps'. In the front line of defence would be 'John and Mary Citizen'.

The exhibition helped to plug the gaps in East Ham's Civil Defence programme. Over 50,000 passed by Britannia and her acolytes and subsequently there were 2000 enrolments in the ARP.

On 11 August the Home Office mounted a trial of the blackout in London. It attracted thousands of sightseers, who treated the event as if it was an entertainment rather than a preparation for war. Alex Glendenning reported the trial for the *Nineteenth-Century Review* from his vantage point at Piccadilly Circus:

> What I had hoped for was a sudden inky plunge as the clock hand touched the half hour (12.30 a.m.) but the authorities were not concerned for dramatic effect and the darkness came gradually. Leicester Square and Shaftesbury Avenue were already doused and here and there a lamp went off in Piccadilly until only the big triple-headed lamps in the Circus itself remained alight. Just before they went out I was moved off the island by a policeman and when the final plunge came the crowd went Ooooh! I was standing among the bonnets of taxicabs and missed the drama.

Scuffles broke out all round the intrepid Glendenning and 'One recalled vaguely that sandbags were once used for other purposes than ARP.'

In East Ham the *Echo* reporter who toured the borough by car during the trial found it

> a strange but not unpleasant experience. The darkness was by no means as black as had been expected, since the stars made an unexpected appearance, quite a few lights were still about in various places in spite of appeals, and there was a surprising amount of reflected light from the numerous searchlights. . . . One warden reported that the only light which he found on in a certain street proved to be that of a room occupied by a loving couple. He is still puzzling over the strange ways of the human mind since, in his own words, 'I should have thought they would have been among those who would have most welcomed the opportunity to switch out their lights!' . . . Shopkeepers of the borough generally cooperated well by extinguishing their usual display lights and there were no incidents like one at Ilford, where one shop's bright display caused an angry crowd to gather

and to take matters into their own hands by smashing the windows and the lights. . . . In all, the control centre at the Town Hall was connected by phone to 43 posts, covering the borough in 228 sectors. Roughly speaking, the posts were on the sites of permanent concrete posts which it is hoped to build shortly. The centre was a hive of activity as messages were received from and sent to all posts.

By the end of the month blackout procedure was being modified. Council workers were out in force, painting white bands round all posts, boxes and other obstacles along important streets, and picking out kerbs and crossways with white markings. All traffic lights were now fitted with blackout shields, which allowed only a small cross of light to be seen instead of the usual full circle.

Armed guards with TA (Territorial Army) armbands were posted on a number of railway bridges in East Ham. On Monday, 28 August, several West Ham United football stars wearing their Territorial Army uniforms turned up to watch a match against Fulham. On the previous weekend the East Ham Borough Council had held an evacuation rehearsal for 10,000 children. The *Echo* reported that a Manor Park woman, charged with shoplifting at East Ham Police Court, blamed her lapse on the world crisis and fear that one of her sons would be called up.

Seemingly unaffected by the world crisis was Lucille Beaumont, the fashion correspondent of the *Echo*'s woman's page, who on the eve of war told her readers, 'Autumn is almost here, and with a shock we realize that we "have not a rag to wear". Our menfolk may moan and groan, but with the approach of the new season, we feel an urge to go out and get ourselves something fresh to wear.'

The Second World War was now almost here. On 23 August came the announcement of the non-aggression pact signed between Germany and the Soviet Union. The next day Parliament was recalled from its summer holiday and military reservists were called up. Members of the Auxiliary Air Service and Volunteer Reserve received green envelopes bearing the word 'MOBILIZATION' in large letters, a lapse of security only partially rectified by heavy overstamping. Visitors to the Royal Air Force Club in Piccadilly noted with surprise the floods of telegrams which threatened to engulf the entrance.

On 25 August Britain signed a formal treaty of alliance with Poland, whose integrity against aggression Prime Minister Neville Chamberlain had informally guaranteed on 31 March. On the 31st *The Times* carried an article 'From Our Own Rugby Correspondent', previewing the 1939–40 season which he confidently believed lay ahead: 'The visit of a fully representative side from Australia and the renewal of relations with France promise to make the rugby season both crowded and one to remember. . . . It is possible that an extra fixture or two may be arranged across the Channel, where also a number of English clubs will hope to renew old associations.' An extra fixture was indeed arranged across the Channel that winter but not the sort *The Times*'s man had in mind.

At 4.15 a.m. on 3 September German troops moved into Poland. Within two hours bombs were falling on Warsaw. In a cotton mill in Bolton, Lancashire, the news was broken by 'a woman hairdresser in Derby Street coming into the mill to tell the manager, who told an oiler and a greaser, who came around telling various weavers. . . . Some believed the news, and some didn't. Then one or two went out of the mill and bought a special. Then they all believed it. One weaver had hysterics.

Opposite, top: Workmen painting a traffic island in Whitehall as part of the blackout precautions taken as war approached. *Opposite, bottom:* Polish troops move up to the border. Poland had begun to mobilise in July 1939, but was to be overwhelmed by the German Wehrmacht in a campaign lasting barely six weeks.

Above: It's official – the headlines tell the bleak story.

Throughout the early summer of 1939 the British man, and woman, in the street maintained their characteristic stoicism as the war clouds gathered, and continued to take no chances when dressing for a day out on the beach.

Opposite, top: The sheet music for 'We'll Meet Again', soon to become one of the most evocative songs of the war.

She had a son. A few were crying, but on the whole they didn't bother much, till about four o'clock, when the boys got their calling papers at the mill. At four o'clock they were all working. At five they were in uniform waiting for their pay. The oldest was only twenty-four. They were all given a hearty send-off. They had a mixture of bravado and fear on their faces.'

The British government, impaled on a pledge to Poland which it had no way of honouring militarily, flapped around feebly in search of a way out. By 2 September the majority of Members of Parliament and the nation were convinced that war was inevitable. When the Conservative MP Henry 'Chips' Channon, an arch-appeaser, attempted to argue with his Party's Chief Whip, he was given the bland reply, 'It must be war, Chips old boy, there's no other way out.'

Still Neville Chamberlain vacillated. That night his Cabinet staged a sit-down strike, refusing to disperse until a decision had been made. After an agonizing silence, Chamberlain said quietly, 'Right gentlemen, this means war.' Almost immediately there was a huge clap of thunder followed by a torrential downpour, a harbinger of the man-made storm which was to hit London in September 1940 when the Blitz began.

Sunday dawned warm and sunny. At 9 a.m. the British ambassador in Berlin presented Hitler with an ultimatum demanding an answer within two hours. No answer was received. At 11.15 a.m. Neville Chamberlain lugubriously broadcast to the nation that 'we are now at war with Germany'.

2
THE PHONEY WAR

We're gonna hang out the washing on the Siegfried Line
Have you any dirty washing, Mother dear?
We're gonna hang out the washing on the Siegfried Line
'Cos the washing day is here.

On Sunday, 3 September 1939, Joan Wildish, an artist's model, wrote in her diary:

> I attended church at 10.30 a.m. The silence was unearthly. No one spoke. We just sat or knelt quietly. Minutes ticked by and then at 11 a.m. the vicar started our service. Almost immediately, the verger hurried down the nave holding a small piece of paper. We all knew what that meant. Our vicar, an elderly man who had been shellshocked in the trenches in the last war, mounted the pulpit and said in a voice that was almost inaudible, 'We are now at war with Germany. We will return to our homes.' He gave the Blessing, and then the congregation walked out in absolute silence. As we left the church the unfamiliar sound of the air-raid warning warbled louder and louder until we felt that we just couldn't stick it. Some returned to the church, others went home. Nothing happened and in a few minutes a car rushed by with a large notice on it saying 'All clear'. The relief was such that I felt the war must be over already.

The false alarm had been raised by a single French aircraft crossing the Channel. The RAF fighters which were scrambled to meet the imaginary threat engaged each other by mistake and two aircraft were shot down in what became ironically known as 'The Battle of Barking Creek'. In the streets of London civilians were shepherded into air-raid shelters by ARP wardens and policemen. The mood was self-consciously calm and orderly, but here and there individuals succumbed to a mixture of excitement and panic. A Mass-Observer* noted:

> Turned on the wireless and I was on the point of sitting down for a well-earned rest [he had been putting up his blackout curtains] when pandemonium suddenly broke out – the wailing of hundreds of sirens in torment. I was filled with with an ecstasy of *exquisite and thrilling panic* – it was war then, or war and an air raid to coincide with it, or even an air raid forestalling a declaration of war.
> I rushed frantically up and down the house, throwing hard-boiled eggs and pyjamas into a suitcase, dashed down to the garage, leapt into the car, and drove it with such abandon that I buckled a wing and had to go forward again before I could extricate it – all to the accompaniment of terrifying siren blasts. I shouted to the wardens who were rushing past to inquire what it signified, thinking it might be the way of signifying war, but was told, 'It's an air raid', and immediately had visions of the wave upon wave of German bombers which we had been told to expect ushering in their idea of 'lightning war'. Meanwhile I careered madly up to Holland Park Avenue till a warden forcibly directed me into Ladbroke Grove and made me take cover, which I did in a garage with a skylight and open front!

*Mass-Observation was founded in 1937 by a young and radical group which included Humphrey Jennings, Tom Harrisson, Kathleen Raine and William Empson. Their aim was to conduct a massive investigation into all aspects of British social life, and one of their first projects was a study of Bolton and Blackpool, the Worktown Project. In the war the running of Mass-Observation was centralized in London and in 1940–41 the group worked in cooperation with the Ministry of Information. After the formal relationship came to an end Mass-Observation continued to provide several government departments with information for the duration of the war. Its observers and interviewers, busily taking notes of the passing scene, often fell under suspicion of being fifth columnists.

After some minutes I thought I heard the all-clear, so got into the car and dashed on to the convent. When I had almost arrived there, I was again stopped by a warden and told to take cover. I and a party of civilians accordingly knocked at the door of one house but the good woman refused admission. Whereupon the warden rushed up in a frenzy of rage and nearly pulverized her, and she promptly collapsed and led us all down to a most evil-smelling basement, where we waited for quarter of an hour or so before the all-clear was given.

On arriving at the station I found everybody standing to their stretchers, fully equipped in anti-gas clothing, and not only ready but expecting to be sent out at any moment. I was told to rush and get a steel helmet and service respirator, then there was *no* spare equipment, so a helmet was snatched off the first man we came to and crammed on my head. I was told to take my civilian respirator and as I had in my car topboots and mackintosh I was soon more or less suitably arrayed for the fray and 'stood by' in my car with engine periodically ticking over, ready to dash a stretcher party to the scene of action when the call came.

Actually nothing happened and by 1 o'clock the alarm was quite over. I learnt then for the first time that Germany had been given a real ultimatum expiring at 11 o'clock that morning.

In the Northeast a young man was out walking in the country with his fiancée when the Gateshead siren sounded in the distance. Calling to his dog, he attempted to steer a course towards a nearby ditch without changing pace. However, his fiancée realized that something was amiss. His explanation produced 'consternation and tears, partly my fault'. A mother out for a country walk with her children was told of the alert by a passing motorist. Expecting an immediate raid – the 'knock-out blow' – she stayed by a ditch at the side of the road, tearing out 'handfuls of grass, thinking I would push the children down there and hide them'. In Croydon, Surrey, a female civil servant recalled feeling 'a bit funky for a while', but carried on washing clothes with her mother. Looking up at the clear blue sky she thought, 'What a sin to start a war on such a beautiful day.' She noticed her neighbours taking shelter in their newly erected Anderson and motionless figures in the street staring up, eyes shielded, into the sky.

The false alarm set the tone of what was to become known as the Phoney War. The declaration of war had released people from an almost unbearable tension. Now there was anticlimax and a feeling of unreality. The mood in Britain at the beginning of the war was captured in a short documentary film produced by Alberto Cavalcanti for the GPO Film Unit. *The First Days* shows the population of London reacting to war with characteristic mildness and restraint. A small group of suburbanites huddle round a car to listen to Chamberlain's announcement. Barrage balloons rise slowly into the sky. When the first sirens sound, people file obediently into the shelters, supervised by wardens whose 'principal equipment is friendliness, the wartime equipment of all Londoners'. A street-corner sandbag shelter in the East End is called the 'Rock of Gibraltar' and decorated with a model cannon and cheerfully insulting messages for Hitler. Perhaps most moving is the quiet, restrained 'goodbye' which the commentator repeats three times over scenes of departing troops. *The First Days* ends with a shot of a diffident barrage balloon drifting off the screen into a cloudy sky, a suitably uncertain image for an uncertain period.

The first major upheaval of the war was set in motion by the government on 1 September. Plans for the evacuation of mothers and children

from danger to reception areas had been laid long before the war, and there had been a small-scale evacuation at the time of the Munich crisis. Now it was for real.

It was by no means a uniform operation across the nation. Some cities which were subsequently heavily bombed, notably Plymouth, Swansea and Bristol, were not designated as evacuation areas. Nor did all the 'priority classes' choose to be evacuated. In London fewer than half the capital's schoolchildren were evacuated; only 25 per cent from the Black Country; and a mere 15 per cent from Sheffield. The government had planned to move about 3,500,000 people, but only about 1,500,000 responded to the official scheme.

This was still a huge operation, described by the Minister of Health, Walter Elliott, as an 'exodus bigger than that of Moses. It is the movement of ten armies, each of which is as big as the whole of the Expeditionary Force.'

The foot soldiers in these armies were children. In the first great wave of evacuation were 827,000 schoolchildren and 524,000 under school age accompanied by their mothers; there were also 12,000 expectant mothers and 103,000 teachers and helpers. The nine-year-old Derek Lambert 'paraded with the other children from Tollington School outside Hornsey station as heavily loaded as a soldier in full marching kit. A gas mask in a white tin box stuffed with sticky plaster, anti-burn cream and iodine pulled me down on one side, a haversack crammed with sandwiches and apples balanced me on the other. Brown paper parcels hung from my belt like grenades – emergency sandwiches, spare socks if

Opposite, top: Ambivalent image of the Phoney War – smartly dressed patrons of London's Paradise Club take shelter during an air raid alert in October 1939. *Opposite, bottom:* Gas masks and dominoes in an Anderson shelter, as yet bare of the homely touches added by most families during the Blitz. *Above, left and right:* What the well-dressed gas mask owner was wearing in the early months of the war.

my feet got wet, a mackintosh cape, a slab of chocolate. In my pocket were labels displaying my school, home address and destination; in one hand I carried a brown suitcase containing clothes, in the other a wad of comics.'

Evacuation provided photographers with some of the most evocative images of the early war years: heart-rending pictures of tearful little scraps, labels around their necks, gas-mask holders strung from their shoulders, teddy bears clutched in grubby little hands, their lips quivering with a mixture of excitement and apprehension. For many it was a profoundly frightening experience. The cartoonist Mel Calman recalled his experiences as an evacuee:

I have this image of a small boy with a label tied round his neck. The boy has no features and is crying. He is carrying a cardboard box, which contains his gas mask.

I remember that labels with our names on were pinned to our clothes before we left London. I think I felt that I had no identity and was a parcel being posted to the country. The labels frightened me as much as the idea of leaving my parents. A child of seven, if lost, can tell people his name. A label assumes that he does not know his name or, worse, has no name and has been given one at random from a list of names.

Perhaps the gas mask felt like a second face, a mask that would replace my own face as soon as I left London. I remember that the gas mask looked inhuman with its celluloid eyeshield and metal snout. I remember that it smelt of rubber and that I could not breathe properly inside it. The shield misted over with condensation and it felt warm and suffocating inside this second face.

I know that we rehearsed the evacuation every morning for a week. Each morning my sister and I would leave home with our packed sandwiches and clothes. We would say goodbye to our parents. Our labels were pinned on and I felt sick. We were not told the date of the real departure in case the Germans bombed the train. That seems hard to believe now, but at that time people seemed to find spies under their beds every night. So we had to leave home without knowing if we would return that day or not. We went through this awful ritual of goodbye every morning for a week. Every morning I felt sick and kissed my parents and felt I was leaving my name and identity with them.

Newspaper photographs of the period portray a deceptively calm and orderly picture of the evacuation. But there was much muddle and confusion. At the beginning of their journey many children were bundled on to waiting trains with scant regard for their eventual destination. Some reception areas were swamped with evacuees; others received only a fraction of the numbers for which they had prepared. Often children arrived dirty, hungry and distressed to find that their billetors were only prepared to accept the most tidily turned out. A kind of auction frequently ensued. Mrs Clara Milburn, a middle-class housewife who lived near Coventry, described the scene at her local school playground in a diary entry of 3 September:

We allotted children to foster parents as we consulted our survey books, took their names and went with them into a schoolroom where they were given a card to be handed to their foster parents, who later signed it as having received them. 'Please, Miss,' (!) one voice said, 'Sydney wants to be with his sister – he's only seven and she looks after him and puts him to bed.' What was to be done? Nobody in small cottage homes could put up a boy and a girl. But at last one of the billeting wardens said she could take

Above: Evacuees set off with a smile, but there were to be many tears later. *Opposite, top:* Enduring image of the war; troops begin one journey, evacuees another in the spring of 1940. *Opposite, bottom:* Hello, Mum! Evacuees greet their mothers in Nottingham, December 1939. One side-effect of evacuation was the disruption of many children's education, a problem compounded by the destruction in the Blitz of many of Britain's schools.

Sydney – two boys instead of one – and Gwen, his sister, could be next door, where another billeting warden wanted 'a nice clean little girl to be with mine – and I *must* take one home today or my little girl will be so disappointed.'

Culture shock was the keynote of the first days of evacuation. The majority of the evacuees were the children of the urban poor, some of them from very deprived homes and afflicted with head lice, a problem exacerbated by the fact that the evacuation had taken place during the school holidays. Often their clothes were wholly unsuitable for a prolonged stay in the country – their parents could afford no better. Many were taken into middle-class homes were mutual incomprehension resulted in much unhappiness for the children and anguish for their hosts.

Some of the poorest evacuees, used to sharing their parents' bed (or even sleeping under it), were nonplussed when faced with new sleeping arrangements. In York the brother of James Agate, the drama critic, reported of some evacuees from Durham: 'They refuse to sleep in a bed. They will sleep under it. . . . Beds, they say, are for dead people – they aren't going to be laid out yet.' Sometimes sorely tried middle-class sensibilities spilled over into class hatred. In his wartime diary James Agate included an extract from a letter written by a friend in the country: 'There are six evacuated children in our house. My wife and I hate them so much that we have decided to *take away* something from them at Christmas.'

The *East Ham Echo*'s letters pages for September 1939 are filled with suspiciously happy and articulate news from evacuees full of the joys of country life. Nearer the mark, perhaps, is the poignant note sent to a mum on the government-issued postcard which notified parents of the children's safe arrival:

Dear Mum,
    I hope you are well. I don't like the man's face much. Perhaps it will look better in the daylight. I like the dog's face best.

Other children found themselves in circumstances so different from their lives at home that it seemed as if they had been transported to a different planet. The thirteen-year-old Bernard Kops and his sister were evacuated from Stepney to prosperous Buckinghamshire. Brother and sister refused to be separated and it was nearly midnight before a house was found for them. 'Rose whispered. . . . She whispered for days. Everything was so clean in the room. We were even given flannels and toothbrushes. We'd never cleaned our teeth up till then. And hot water came from the tap. And there was a lavatory upstairs. And carpets. And something called an eiderdown. This was all very odd. And rather scaring.'

Derek Lambert exchanged life in a suburban semi for the strange new delights of the countryside.

Our foster parents took their new duties seriously. They were godfearing, clean and healthy, and they led us in the ways of godliness, cleanliness and good health.
    Mr Storey was young and strong, with glistening dark hair, sinewed forearms and reserves of patience as deep as the village pond. He wore dark blue overalls, worked as a mechanic and played cricket every summer Saturday. . . .

Sometimes Mr Storey took us on a rabbit shoot with his friends and a black and white clown of a dog called Toby. . . .

Mrs Storey did her best to warm the strangeness around us and prevent the bouts of night-time despair. She was gentle and worried and, like my mother, had dietary remedies for all ills. They all originated in the garden – in bags of mint, wafers of onion, rubbings of chives, sniffs of rosemary and lavender. But her real panacea was a full belly. And the first return of vague security centred around heaps of garden potatoes, garden carrots and garden parsnips almost hiding the meat of the rabbit. . . .

Another factor which charmed us into accepting our new way of life was sanitation. There was no chain, no cistern: it was hardly credible, rather disgusting, decidely intriguing.

It was with something approaching shock that many well-to-do foster parents were brought face to face with the extent of urban poverty in Britain. The MP Oliver Lyttelton, who was soon to join the government, had volunteered to put up ten evacuees in his country home and had received thirty-one. He wrote: 'I got a shock . . . I had little dreamt that English children could be so completely ignorant of the simplest rules of hygiene, and that they would regard the floors and carpets as possible places on which to relieve themselves.' In a private letter Neville Chamberlain confessed: 'I never knew that such conditions existed, and I feel ashamed of having been so ignorant of my neighbours.' Evacuation threw many social problems into sharp relief and undoubtedly had a profound effect on the shifts in social policy which were to take place during the war and were to shape the Beveridge Report, published in December 1942.

In spite of the unfamiliar surroundings and separation from their parents, many children adapted happily to life in the country. A famous *Punch* cartoon of April 1940 showed an evacuee greeting her visiting mother with the words, 'This is spring, Mummy, and they have one every year down here.' By then, however, three out of every four evacuees had returned home. There had been no bombing, and to this was added homesickness and a government demand for a small parental contribution towards the upkeep of the evacuated children. The government tried to stem the tide with a publicity campaign. Posters showed a worried-looking mother sitting beneath a tree surrounded by her children. In the distance are the smoking chimneys of the city, while behind her a spectral Adolf Hitler whispers into her ear, 'Take them back, take them back, take them back.' But take them back the mothers did. A new evacuation scheme launched by the government in February 1940 was a complete failure. It was planned to move 670,000 children, without their mothers, if heavy raids were launched by the Germans. All children would undergo a complete medical check-up before departure; parents would register in advance and undertake not to bring their children home. But by the end of April only one householder in fifty was prepared to offer a billet in the designated reception areas, and barely 20 per cent of parents in the evacuation areas had registered for the scheme.

There had been other evacuations at the beginning of the war. Nearly 3000 children were evacuated to the United States and Canada, an operation which was brought to an abrupt end when a U boat torpedoed the evacuation ship *City of Benares* with the loss of seventy-three 'seavacuees'. Civilian institutions, including the BBC and government departments, were evacuated to 'safe' areas. The BBC Variety Department was sent to Bristol and its headquarters established at a country house near Evesham, where its security-conscious employees patrolled the grounds at night armed with wooden clubs. The National Gallery sent its treasures to a cave in a disused slate quarry in north Wales. The newly created Ministry of Food was based in Colwyn Bay. Anticipating a flood of air-raid casualties, the government largely cleared the great London hospitals of their patients and evacuated most of the staff to the country. Some 2,000,000 individuals evacuated themselves, many of them to private hotels and guest houses, popularly dubbed 'funk holes', far from the blasts of war. In January 1941 *The Times* devoted an editorial to castigating the country hotels 'filled with well-to-do refugees, who often have fled from nothing. They sit and read and knit and eat and drink and get no nearer the war than the news they read in the newspapers.'

Animals, too, were evacuated. In September 1939 a *Times* advertisement offered 'a few approved dogs full board and country walks; gas-proof dug-out and every care for 15s a week.' An ARP radio broadcast of the early months of the war advised pet-owners: 'Send your pets to the country if you can. If you cannot, remember that your dog will not be allowed to go into a public air-raid shelter with you. So don't take him shopping with you. Take him for walks near home, so that you can get back quickly. When you take him into your own shelter with you, put him on a lead. If you can get a muzzle for him, you should do so, because he may get hysterical during raids. Put some cotton wool in his ears. Ask your chemist to mix a dose of bromide all ready for you to give him when an air raid starts. Don't worry about your cats. Cats can take care of themselves far better than you can. Your cat will probably meet you when you get into the shelter.' In spite of these reassuring words, many a Rover, and a Tiddles, went to the lethal chamber at the beginning of the war.

Friday, 1 September, also brought the blackout. There had been a rush to the shops to buy blinds, curtains, blackout paint, cardboard, brown paper and drawing pins, all of which quickly became virtually unobtainable. The blackout problems of the individual householder paled into insignificance compared to those which faced large firms: it cost £12,000 for HMV to black out its factory at Hayes; a city textile firm, with fifty big skylights, needed 8,000 square yards of material.

In both town and country the blackout transformed Britain's night-time landscape. A Yorkshireman recalled walking on the moorland ridge above his house: 'At night in clear weather, while the hills and coastline would have been blurred, I could have picked out every individual farm and village in that landscape and, especially in the holiday season, the lights of Whitby and Scarborough would have made a big yellow glow in the sky. Now, although the weather was fine, there was not a pinprick of light anywhere, not even on the sea.' The *Illustrated London News* welcomed the blackout in London, celebrating the capital as 'the new Rome', bathed in 'moonlit scenes of mystic calm'. However, for most people the blackout was an infernal nuisance, and a bigger menace to civilian lives than the war in Europe. In East Ham in September the number of road accidents nearly tripled; even in December, when people had adjusted to picking their way through the blackout, there were seven fatalities in one week. Walking home from the pub at closing time became a journey fraught with peril.

On 6 October the indefatigable Lucille Beaumont rallied to the cause in the *East Ham Echo*'s woman's page with advice on:

Your Blackout Suit

Three-piece suits are particularly suitable because of their versatility. They'll look good three years from now, and women are buying them in the best quality they can afford, realizing that they may have to wear them as long as that. . . . 'Blackout' fashions are no longer confined to white belts and berets. You can now buy artificial gardenias treated with luminous paint. During the day no one would suspect that they were other than very attractive accessories, but at night they gleam in our darkened streets as effectively as the reflector-studded white belts that you buy in the West End stores.

The same month the *Observer* noted: 'Marshall and Snelgrove are having a great success with their blackout coats for dogs. Costing half a guinea, they are made in white gleaming fabric (with an occasional red spot) . . . with bells to announce his coming. Add, too, your dog's identity disc, and even if he should stray, you can feel that he is safe.'

Night trains, already slow, crowded and deprived of restaurant cars, ran with the blinds drawn, each compartment illuminated by a blue pinpoint which barely allowed travellers to distinguish the features of their fellow-passengers. The windows of tube trains and buses were covered to protect passengers from flying glass in the event of the windows being shattered by a bomb blast; there was a small diamond slit in the texture to allow passengers to identify stations and stops as they flashed by. The Stygian gloom inside a bus during the blackout made it extremely difficult for the conductor to distinguish between silver and copper, encouraging much passing of dud coins.

A letter to *The Times* of 8 November 1939 offered some useful advice on how best to negotiate the blackout:

When walking in the blackout, whichever side of the pavement they take, walkers are involved in unexpected risks: on the one side Belisha beacons, lamp-posts, pillar boxes and sand bins; on the other, sandbag promontories. The middle of the pavement is the only safe place and . . . I suggest that the better rule at night would be that walkers northwards should use the west and those walking southward the east pavement. . . . It does not matter which side of the street one walks since there are no shops or other attractions.

Modifications were gradually introduced to mitigate the hazards of the strict blackout. From mid-October 1939 pedestrians were able to use hand torches provided they were muffled by two thicknesses of tissue paper and were turned off in a raid. Civilian drivers were permitted to fit masked headlights, made compulsory in 1940, which allowed a thin beam through a narrow horizontal slit. By Christmas 1939 the partial illumination of churches, markets and street stalls was permitted, and a little light allowed in shop windows. Some towns introduced 'glimmer lighting' at road junctions and selected points, in which a streetlight directed a pinprick of light down to the pavement.

As days turned into weeks the dreaded aerial bombardment failed to materialize. The 150,000 troops of the British Expeditionary Force (BEF) which had crossed to France saw no action. Visiting the front line, Prime Minister Neville Chamberlain asked querulously, 'The Germans don't want to attack do they?' It was not until December that the British sustained their first casualty, one Corporal T. W. Priday, whose patrol had the misfortune to bump unexpectedly into some Germans. The first civilian victim of an air raid was an Orkneyman, Jim Isbister, who died during an air raid on the naval base at Scapa Flow on 16 March 1940.

Right: Low's famous cartoon creation, the irascible Colonel Blimp, delivers a crusty riposte to the blackout in the offices of Penguin Books. *Far right, top:* A farmer's wife takes drastic measures to ensure the safety of one of her herd. *Far right, centre:* Some householders coated the keyholes in their front doors with luminous paint to avoid frustrating minutes fumbling in the dark. *Below:* A poster provides a complete run-down of all the blackout precautions to be taken by the prudent motorist.

Above: Housewives cast a sceptical eye over blackout material. It soon became difficult to find. At the end of September 1939 *Woman's Own* suggested masking lights by fitting a cocoa tin with a hole cut in the base, giving sufficient light to read by, or painting light bulbs with Reckitt's Blue mixed with water – 'Incidentally, the blue can be washed off instantly when the war is over.' *Right:* Two pedestrians put their shirt tails to good use, making themselves as conspicuous as possible while strolling home in the blackout.

Right: An air spotter keeps a weather eye open for enemy raiders during a soccer match between Arsenal and Charlton Athletic at the Charlton ground in December 1940. During the war professional football was reorganised on a regional basis, to save travelling time, and crowds were initially restricted by ARP regulations to one-eighth of their peacetime capacity. The call-up inevitably affected the standard of League games, but the football stars in the services were kept busy in representative games.

There was an air of unreality about the war. RAF Bomber Command was dropping propaganda leaflets rather than bombs on Germany. The savage winter weather of 1939–40 was a greater threat to the aircrew than the enemy's air defences. Inches of snow built up on the control surfaces, airspeed indicators froze up and oxygen supplies failed. Some crews resorted to battering their heads on the floor or the navigation table to seek distraction from the cold.

Many of the leaflets they dropped were ingenious, although their effect on the German population was not discernible. The pamphlets dropped on Berlin on the night of 1–2 October 1939 provided citizens of the German capital with detailed information about the personal fortunes salted away abroad by the Nazi leaders. These revelations failed to shame Hitler and his henchmen into surrender. The future C-in-C of Bomber Command, Air Marshal Sir Arthur Harris, drily observed at the time that the only usefulness of the leaflet campaign was to provide the people of Germany with several years' free toilet paper.

Below: An early casualty of war – curious civilians inspect a German He111 bomber brought down on a Scottish moor in October 1939.

The War Cabinet was most reluctant to initiate a full-scale air war of the kind which had been envisaged in the 1930s. To a suggestion that the RAF might bomb the industrial region of the Ruhr, the Air Minister, Sir Kingsley Wood, made the now famous remark that this was quite out of the question as the Ruhr's factories were private property.

There were alarms and excitements: in October the battleship *Royal Oak* was sunk at Scapa Flow by a U-boat; in December the German pocket battleship *Graf Spee* was scuttled off Montevideo; in February 1940 came the freeing of the prisoners aboard the German supply ship *Altmark*, a coup which won considerable credit for the First Lord of the Admiralty, Winston Churchill. Nevertheless, the Phoney War seemed to be an affair run not by soldiers but by conscientious civil servants. It was a war of red tape rather than bombs. The mood was caught in the very first broadcast, on 19 September 1939, of Tommy Handley's radio show 'It's That Man Again', with Handley's installation as the Minister of Aggravation in the Office of Twerps. He summons his secretary:

> TOMMY: Take a memo: 'To all concerned in the Office of Twerps: Take notice that from today, September the twenty-tooth, I, the Minister of Aggravation, have power to confiscate, complicate and commandeer –
> VERA: How do you spell 'commandeer', Mr Hanwell?
> TOMMY: Commandeer – let me see. [*Sings*] Comm-om-and-ear, comm-on-and-ear, Tommy Handley's wag-time band, comm-on-and-ear, etc. Er, where were we? I have the power to seize anything on sight.
> VERA: Oh, Mr Handpump – and me sitting so close to you!

Fewer and fewer people now went out with their gas masks. The cinemas and theatres, closed on the outbreak of war, were quickly reopened and were soon doing a brisk trade. Rationing had not yet been introduced, although prices were beginning to climb steeply. Clothing was up by some 25 per cent, and Mass-Observation recorded a housewife's comment that 'a kettle half the size of one I used to buy at Woolworth's for 6d now costs 10d, candles which used to cost 10d a packet now cost between 1s 6d and 1s 8d'.

Below, left: Going up. Looking strangely out of place in a suburban setting, a barrage balloon is readied to float aloft. At the beginning of the war it took a crew of two corporals and eight men at least 40 minutes to raise a barrage balloon. In the early days balloon crews were often accommodated in huts and – in a homely touch – fed on rations supplied in hayboxes from a central kitchen. From 1941 women of the WAAF began to take over the flying of balloons. *Below, right:* Going down. Piccadilly Circus' Eros was put into storage for the duration and only returned to its pedestal in 1946.

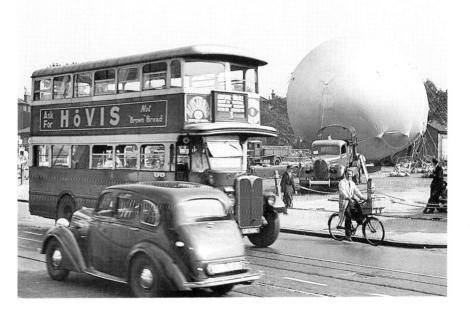

A gas-powered car lumbers through the streets. The bag and auxiliary carburettor to run your car on unrationed town gas cost £30. But the gas bag made the car very difficult to handle, and its 202 cubic feet of gas was the equivalent of only one gallon of petrol (in terms of the war effort, a Lancaster bomber required 2,000 gallons of petrol to reach the Rühr). By the autumn of 1942 the gas-powered car had disappeared from the roads. On the left is the trailer of a gas-powered bus.

Unemployment, the scourge of the 1930s, was still running at over a million by April 1940. And there were twenty different makes of car on the market, some of them new models. However, the petrol to power them was in short supply. Rationing had been introduced in September, leading to a boom in bicycles and a brief vogue for gas-powered vehicles, their fuel housed in billowing sacks on their roofs. In March 1942 the abolition of the civilian 'basic' petrol ration took most people's cars off the road for the duration. Commercial petrol was dyed red, and if the police found traces of red in the engine of a non-commercial vehicle, the owner could be heavily fined. There was a thriving black market, for it was a relatively simple matter to remove the red dye.

The British are, perhaps, the greatest grumblers in the world, raising the national habit of moaning almost to the level of an art form. One American journalist despaired of the British, who seemed to treat the war as an endless series of small personal affronts rather than a national struggle for survival. In November 1939 Mass-Observation compiled a list of the nation's principal grumbles, taking the blackout as a universal standard of annoyance at 100:

Main grumbles	Town	Country
Blackout	100	100
Food	66	68
Fuel, petrol	44	50

Evacuation	37	64
Prices	42	39
Lack of amusements	30	21
Transport	38	14
Lack of news	36	21

Grumbling apart, war for many seemed like 'business as usual'. Advertisements in the *East Ham Echo* began to take on wartime themes. As early as 15 September Woodmansee's appealed to the parents of evacuated children with 'Long Life Clothes for the Children Away'. T. S. Thomas and Co. of Plasket Grove, East Ham, were advertising complete ARP sets, including 'Incendiary Shovel, Hoe, Bucket and Sand (as recommended by the Home Office Pamphlet)'. Readers were assured that 'in times of stress' Guinness was good for settling the nerves. In December an advertisement appeared inquiring,

Can Your Tommy Ask for Roast Beef in French? There's a thousand times when he'll bless you for sending him a copy of this wonderful English-French phrase book! He doesn't have to speak a word of French; he looks up the English phrase, such as 'What is the time?' and there he has the French equivalent in such a way that he has only to read it out, i.e. 'Kell err ay teel?' This is French made simple. Here's the very best turn you can possibly do for your man – FRENCH AS YOU MARCH, 1s.

In the early months of 1940 the press gave considerable coverage to the feeling that a 'creeping paralysis' was enveloping the British war effort under Neville Chamberlain's government. Suddenly, in April 1940, the war lurched into life. On the 4th Neville Chamberlain confidently announced: 'Hitler has missed the bus.' Within a week the Führer had occupied Denmark and invaded Norway. An attempt by the British and French to land and maintain an expeditionary force in Norway ended in disaster. On 8 May there was a debate in the House of Commons on the Norwegian debacle. Leo Amery, addressing the government, said, 'In the name of God, go!' Chamberlain, now grievously afflicted by cancer, resigned and was succeeded on 10 May by Winston Churchill. In truth, Churchill bore a heavy responsibility for the fiasco in Norway, but the hour had brought forth the man. The effect of his unique and combative personality was a factor which Hitler could not have anticipated. As he went to bed in the small hours of the 11th, Churchill was 'conscious of a profound sense of relief. At last I had the authority to give directions over the whole scene. I felt as if I were walking with destiny, and that all my past life had been but a preparation for this hour and for this trial. Eleven years in the political wilderness had freed me from ordinary Party antagonisms. My warnings over the last six years had been so numerous, so detailed and were now so terribly vindicated, that no one could gainsay me. I could not be reproached either for making the war or with want of preparation for it. I thought I knew a good deal about it all, and I was sure that I should not fail. Therefore, although impatient for morning, I slept soundly and had no need for cheering dreams. Facts are better than dreams.'

On the day of Churchill's appointment as Prime Minister, Germany attacked Holland and Belgium. Employing Blitzkrieg tactics – rapid tank manoeuvres supported by dive-bombers – the German forces sliced through the French Army, which was led by men expecting a repeat of the attritional war of 1914–18. France's supposedly impregnable Maginot

A policeman wheels his way sedately through the streets with a sign intended to help the hard of hearing.

33

Line, built at colossal expense in the 1930s, counted for nothing as the main German thrust through the Ardennes simply outflanked it. By 14 May German tanks had crossed the River Meuse and were sweeping north to trap huge numbers of French and British troops in northern France and Belgium. German armour reached the Channel on the 20th. That day contingency plans were being drawn up by Admiral Ramsay, Flag Officer at Dover, for the evacuation of the British Expeditionary Force. The operation, Dynamo, was approved by the War Cabinet on the evening of the 26th when Lord Gort, the commander of the BEF, was already withdrawing towards the Channel ports. Initially there were fears that the operation, which began on the night of 27–28 May, would extricate only 35,000 men. When Dynamo ended on the night of 2 June, some 338,000 troops (225,000 of them British) had been taken off the beaches. The majority were picked up by the Royal Navy, but one of the enduring images of the Dunkirk miracle was that of the 'little ships' – from fishing smacks to Southern Railway Channel steamers – which sailed through wrecks and minefields to play their part in the evacuation.

'Bloody Marvellous!' was the *Daily Mirror* headline which greeted the successful completion of Dynamo but, as Churchill told the House of Commons on 4 June, 'wars are not won by evacuations'. The Dunkirk evacuation had saved us from comprehensive and crippling military defeat, but the return of the troops brought the awful reality of war to the nation's doorstep. Nurse K. M. Phipps, employed with the staff of University College, London, at Ashridge Manor in Kent, wrote in her diary:

> Our staff nurse was a bit jittery, her fiancé was with the BEF and some nasty rumours had been floating around to the effect that they were being evacuated under fire! But nobody knew anything definite. . . . Then a car drew up.
>
> Two officers got out limping, and were helped into Ward 10. We were all standing outside the hut door in spite of the sister's feeble suggestion that it would look better if we were inside! Then it dawned on us that indeed things were wrong. . . . The officers were dirty and untidy, one lacked a uniform coat, the other had a bloody sling on his arm. Surely after going through the regular Army casualty routine someone would have cleaned them up! They looked as if they had come straight off the battlefield . . . but we were not a first field dressing post, we were a base hospital . . . the terminal point in fact. What could have happened!

With a terrible rush the war had come to the shores of England. One of the first actions of Churchill's new coalition government had been to pass an amended Emergency Powers (Defence) Act, by which 'all persons could be required to place themselves, their services, and their property' at the disposal of the government as appeared 'to be necessary or expedient for securing the public safety, the defence of the Realm, the maintenance of public order. . . .' Britain's coastline sprouted dense thickets of barbed wire. It became an offence to leave a car unlocked, or to do anything else which might in any way help German parachutists, hordes of whom were daily expected to descend from the sky disguised as nuns. Civilian movement was heavily restricted in the whole southern 'Defence Area'. On 13 June a ban was announced on the ringing of church bells: henceforward they would be rung only by the military and the police to warn that an attack by airborne forces was in progress. To prevent troop movements being hampered by thousands of fleeing civilians – as had happened in France – the inhabitants of potential

Opposite: The erection of one of the infamous brick street shelters. Until they were modified at the height of the Blitz, they remained dank, dirty and dangerous.

Above: With invasion looming, signposts and place-names were removed or painted out in order to confuse the potential invader. The lasting effect was to confuse the British motorist.

invasion areas were told by the government to 'Stay Where You Are'. A public information leaflet, *If the Invader Comes*, warned: 'Do not give the German anything. Do not tell him anything. Hide your food and your bicycles. Hide your maps. . . . Think always of your country before you think of yourself.'

On 18 June, three days before France signed a humiliating armistice with Germany, Winston Churchill broadcast to the nation: 'What General Weygand called the Battle of France is over. I expect that the Battle of Britain is about to begin. . . . Let us therefore brace ourselves to our duties, and so bear ourselves that, if the British Empire and its Commonwealth last for a thousand years, men will still say, "This was their finest hour."'

The Navy's here! A wounded soldier is helped ashore after the Dunkirk evacuation. In all, some 338,000 troops (225,000 of them British) were plucked from the beaches.

3

THE HOME GUARD

The enormous success of the television comedy series 'Dad's Army', launched by the BBC in 1969, has won the Home Guard a special place in the folklore of the war. Its characters have a life of their own: the pompous, inefficient platoon commander, the enthusiastic but decrepit veteran of Queen Victoria's colonial wars, the wide boy dodging more strenuous military service, and the spotty youth barely out of short trousers and barely capable of understanding the simplest orders. 'Dad's Army' painted a warmly affectionate picture of this unique citizen army, with a grounding in fact; there are countless stories about the Home Guard, some of them perhaps apocryphal, which testify to the British eccentricity and dogged determination to 'muddle through'. But amid the comic antics of Walmington-on-Sea's motley Home Guard platoon it is all too easy to forget that in the summer of 1940 these civilian soldiers were preparing to use the few weapons they had against the most efficient mechanized army the world had seen. The invasion never came, but the Home Guard went from strength to strength, playing a vital role throughout the war. It gave many thousands of citizens, who remained in civilian employment, a complete involvement in all aspects of the war effort. In 1940 the Germans dubbed the Home Guard a 'murder band', but Dad's Army had the last laugh.

There's a Home Guard Sentry at the end of Lover's Lane
So it's no place for lovers anymore . . .
And when you say 'Dear Heart, will you be mine?'
Someone answers 'Friend, advance and give the countersign'

On 17 June 1940, three days after the German Army had marched into Paris, the writer A. P. Herbert was trudging past Greenwich on his way to Canvey Island. A tug skipper yelled gaily to him across the water, 'Now we know where we are! No more bloody allies!'

Britain was alone, and the British were in a state bordering on exultation, as if all the misfortunes of the last nine months had been the result of having unreliable allies. Invasion might come at any moment, but even after Dunkirk the British did not feel like a defeated people, although their military resources were slender.

The British Expeditionary Force had abandoned all its heavy equipment in France. The greater part of the forces was overseas – in the Middle East, Gibraltar, Malta, Hong Kong, Singapore, India, Burma and West Africa. There was a desperate shortage of fully trained men. The last formations to join the BEF had themselves been seriously deficient in training and equipment. The 9th Queen's Royal Lancers went into action in France with less than half its paper armoured strength, without any field guns or a proper complement of anti-tank and anti-aircraft guns, without infantry, without air support, without the bulk of its ancillary services, and with part of its headquarters housed in a three-ply wooden 'armoured' command vehicle.

On 8 June, while the BEF was still re-forming, the Army fielded fifteen divisions in the United Kingdom (including one in Northern Ireland) and one armoured division. The average strength of the infantry divisions was 11,000, well below their establishment. Two of them had under-

"Let 'em all come"

MEN
41-55

HOME DEFENCE
BATTALIONS
Apply at any Army Recruiting Centre Now

Eager civilians join that archetypal wartime phenomenon, an orderly queue, to sign up with the Local Defence Volunteers.

taken no divisional training; five had managed only a little; and the rest had worked up to a standard which the War Office considered 'fair'.

Between them these inexperienced formations could muster only fifty-four 2-pounder anti-tank guns, weapons which in France had proved useless against all but the lightest German tanks. The 2300 Bren guns available to them would have equipped barely five divisions. Their 395 light tanks were little more than death traps; of the heavier Cruiser and Infantry tanks there were, respectively, only seventy-two and thirty-three. The Chiefs of Staff were of the opinion that, 'Should the Germans succeed in establishing a force with its vehicles in this country, our army forces have not got the offensive power to drive it out.'

It was in this atmosphere of remarkable moral strength and alarming material weakness that the Home Guard was born. As early as October 1939 Winston Churchill had suggested to the Home Secretary, Sir John Anderson, that a 'Home Guard' of 500,000 men over the age of forty should be formed. In the spring of 1940 a number of enterprising individuals had formed their own private militias. In Herefordshire Lady Helena Gleichen organized eighty of her staff and tenants into the splendidly named 'Much Marcle Watchers' – a name reminiscent of the title of a wartime radio comedy show – and made an unsuccessful appeal to the Army for weapons. Several months before Dunkirk the Bishop of Chelmsford raised a band of 100 armed vigilantes in the Romford area.

On 14 May, as German armour rolled over the bridges thrown across the Meuse, Churchill's new War Secretary, Anthony Eden, spoke on the radio about the threat of German parachutists. He then made this appeal:

> 'Since the war began the Government has received countless inquiries from all over the kingdom from men of all ages who are for one reason or another not at present engaged in military service, and who wish to do something for the defence of their country. Well, now is your opportunity. We want large numbers of such men in Great Britain, who are British subjects, between the ages of 17 and 65 . . . to come forward now and offer their services. . . . The name of the new Force which is now to be raised will be "The Local Defence Volunteers". . . . This name describes its duties in three words. . . . This is a part-time job, so that there will be no need for any volunteer to abandon his present occupation. . . . When on duty you will form part of the armed forces. . . . You will not be paid, but you will receive a uniform and will be armed. . . .'

Before Eden had finished his broadcast, the first Volunteers were arriving at their local police stations. The constabulary were unprepared for such enthusiasm; in one Kentish village the local bobby turned out to deal with what he took to be a mob of illegally armed civilians descending on his station and ordered them to hand over their weapons.

The police quickly ran out of enrolment forms. No one knew what to do with those which had been filled in, as they were to be handed over to a 'properly appointed' commander. No such commanders existed. A solution was found which had been tried and tested 350 years before, when the nation had faced another invasion threat, that of the Armada. The lords lieutenant of the counties were called in and, in concert with the senior army commanders in their areas, set about appointing retired officers as area, zone and group organizers, charged with selecting commanders for their different localities or confirming the choices already made by individual units.

Within twenty-four hours 250,000 men had enrolled in the Local Defence Volunteers (LDV), and by the end of June their numbers had swollen to 1.5 million. In a broadcast of 14 July 1940, Churchill first referred to the new citizen army as 'the Home Guard', and the name stuck. Qualifications required were minimal: as one veteran of the First World War recalled, the Home Guard was the 'complete answer to the "old sweat's prayer"'. There was no medical examination – recruits were required only to be 'capable of free movement'. Experience with weapons was not deemed essential, which led to some hair-raising incidents in the early days. The upper age limit of sixty-five was not strictly observed; the oldest member of the Home Guard was well into his eighties and had first seen action in the Egyptian campaign of 1884–85.

Many of the early recruits were veterans of the First World War. A Berkshire volunteer recalled, 'I think that none of us will forget our first LDV route march. On it a quarter of a century slipped away in a flash. Then came memories of the Menin Road, of loose, shifting, exasperating cobbles, of the smell of cordite and the scream of shrapnel, of the mud and stench and misery of Flanders, of hopes and fears in battles long ago. . . . There were few youngsters in that first platoon of ours.'

A wartime diarist, Mrs Brinton-Lee, whose husband was to become a major in the Home Guard, described the men in his unit in an entry of September 1940:

The LDV armbands worn here date this picture to the early days of the Home Guard, at a time when rifles were a rarity. Many of the armbands were run up by members of the Women's Voluntary Service (WVS).

They were most of them elderly, with kind, careworn faces. I thought how nice they were, neither bombastic or craven, like the Germans I had met. They had done their job in the last war, as their ribbons showed; they had worked and worried and raised their families. The things they were interested in were good things – their work, their hobbies, their children and their sport. They had no inferiority complex, they had never gone hysterical or wished to take away anyone's freedom. Their only crime was that, being unable to believe that the rest of the world was crazy, they had been rather inclined to let things slide. They did not know how to spell Czechoslovakia, or where it was, and they had been only too willing to believe that Europe was no concern of theirs. Now, when they found everything had come unstuck, they turned up quite cheerfully, and offered themselves and their services again. They were tough and uncomplaining. I was sure that they would fight like tigers when it came to the point, and meanwhile they practised their drill and shooting in the friendliest way, and went home to be with their families through the night's hell, till it was time to go to work in the morning.

Anthony Eden had promised the Volunteers that 'you will receive a uniform and will be armed'. At first the only item of uniform was an armband marked 'HG'. Weapons were equally scarce. A public appeal brought in 20,000 firearms, including a number from the gunroom at Sandringham. Only a lucky few, however, were issued with Short Lee Enfield rifles, which had been standard equipment in the First World War. For the rest, improvisation was the order of the day. In Manchester several rifles last fired in the Indian Mutiny were salvaged from the Zoological Gardens. In the props room at the Theatre Royal, Drury Lane, a long-forgotten cache of rusty Lee Enfields was unearthed and pressed into service. In Essex a former naval rating took command of a 'cutlass platoon'. Across the nation Home Guard units mustered clutching a weird assortment of weaponry: assegais brought back from the Zulu Wars, golf clubs, truncheons and, in at least one unit, packets of pepper 'to interfere with the vision of any persistent unwelcome visitor'.

Legend has also equipped the early Home Guard platoons with pikes, lengths of iron tubing with a bayonet-like blade at the end. These were indeed issued, but not until September 1941, when the threat of invasion had passed and the majority of Home Guard units were substantially better equipped. Most platoon commanders banished these embarrassing and quite useless War Office afterthoughts to their store units. One Home Guard officer put the pikes to work, spiking litter after a sports gala.

Of greater practical use was a consignment of 500,000 .300 rifles from the United States which arrived in July. Getting them to the Home Guard was a lengthy business as the rifles had been embalmed in glutinous oil since 1918; in Cambridge it took 250 female volunteers a fortnight to clean a batch of 8000. At this stage in the war the Home Guard's firepower represented a triumph of optimism over operational reality. On 5 June the C-in-C Home Forces, General Sir Edmund Ironside, declared, 'I do not want you to misjudge the shotgun. I have now coming out over a million rounds of solid ammunition, which is something that will kill a leopard at 200 yards.' But it was German armour, rather than big game, which preyed on the minds of most Home Guards.

The first Home Guard patrols were mounted by the Worthing Battalion of the Sussex Home Guard on 15 May. On 17 May Eastern Command issued an order for patrols to be carried out by 1500 Volunteers in Sussex and Kent. In Leeds, No. 2 Platoon of 3 Company was given

the task of guarding the area around the Cobble Hall Golf Club. Captain T. E. Mason recorded their unconventional introduction to war service:

29 May   First guard mounted.
Dress – golf gear
Arms – a stout stick
Guard room – Club lounge. Easy chairs for sleep.
20–31 May   Guard now armed, two members having brought .22 rifles. Had to reprimand one man very severely for rabbiting in the early morning when he ought to have been on the lookout.
31 May   Received 6 SMLE rifles and 100 rds .300 s.a.a. This was red-letter day. The bearing of the men completely changed under the influence of a little arms drill. Club tearoom handed over to us as a permanent guardroom. Drying room given to us 'for the duration' for use as armoury. Blankets, beds, mattresses, gumboots and oilskins given to us by various members of the club who were either too old or already in the CD, services. . . .

We had to stand a lot of chaff from the other platoons because of the rather *de luxe* conditions under which we were doing our guard. The Council and Staff of the Golf Club did everything they could to help, and their attentions were sometimes embarrassing. On one occasion the Orderly Officer (whose own platoon was very badly housed) arrived at 22.30 hours just as a waitress, looking very prim in white cap and apron, brought into the guardroom a tray with sandwiches and coffee, for the Sergeant of the Guard. . . .

'Dad's Army (or perhaps 'Grandad's Army'). Winston Churchill inspects members of the House of Commons Home Guard. Although it never won a battle honour, the Home Guard can claim the distinction of taking prisoner the Deputy Führer of the Third Reich, Rudolf Hess, when on the night of 10/11 May 1941 he baled out of an Me110 which he had piloted to Renfrewshire on a mission which, to this day, remains unexplained.

41

The whimsical guardians of Cobble Hall's fairways, greens and bunkers had been on the lookout for enemy parachutists. The overriding importance attached to the danger of airborne invasion prompted the newspapers to dub the LDV units 'Parashots'. In a broadcast of 16 June J. B. Priestley described a visit to an LDV unit:

> A night or two ago I had my first spell with our Local Defence Volunteers or 'Parashots'. . . . Ours is a small and scattered village, but we'd had a fine response to the call for Volunteers; practically every able-bodied man in the place takes his turn. The post is on top of a high down, with a fine view over a dozen wide parishes. The men I met up there the other night represented a good cross-section of English rural life; we had a parson, a bailiff, a builder, farmers and farm labourers. Even the rarer and fast disappearing rural trades were represented – for we had a hurdle-maker there; and his presence, together with that of a woodman and a shepherd, made me feel sometimes that I'd wandered into one of those rich chapters of Thomas Hardy's fiction in which his rustics meet in the gathering darkness on some Wessex hillside. And indeed there was something in the preliminary talk, before the sentries were posted for the night, that gave this whole horrible business of air raids and threatened invasion a rustic, homely, almost comfortable atmosphere, and really made a man feel more cheerful about it. . . .

In its heroic early days the Home Guard charted an inimitably British course between democracy and anarchy. In the Sussex village of Wilmington, 'shepherds, farmhands, gardeners, village shopkeepers, a retired civil servant from India, a retired schoolteacher, and one or two people who worked in London and had cottages in downland', gathered at the Black Horse pub to form a platoon. A subsidiary meeting was held in a neighbouring hamlet: 'Men came in from their work in the fields, and we stood round a farm waggon in a farmyard and discussed things and elected a local section leader, calling him Corporal. Communications were the difficulty, so we went to the big house of a local colonel to get him to agree to let us use his telephone. The corporal's wife (a domestic there) could answer if need be. . . . Then came the "election of officers". . . . The local section leader must obviously be a chap always there in the village, so the choice fell on Roy, mine host at the pub. "He's the best rabbit shot in the neighbourhood," said one of his backers.'

The choice of the rank of corporal for the section leader may well have been the cause of much agonizing at Wilmington. When the LDV was formed no formal ranks had been envisaged, although this did not prevent numerous retired generals from parading in full regimental glory, weighed down by gongs. In addition to no ranks and no pay, there were virtually no public funds set aside to meet the expenses incurred by the LDV units. Such basic items as blankets, lanterns, typewriters and stationery had to be scrounged. At Wilmington 'our chief observation post was an exposed hilltop, which meant a long walk from the village and a stiff climb at the end. It was all right in the summer, but we felt we should need shelter in the bleak winter. So a deputation went to a gypsy encampment and bargained for an old caravan. We got it, I think, under five pounds, using the funds subscribed in the village. We spent a bit more money on paint for camouflage, which to my mind made the gypsy caravan more conspicuous than ever after our amateur efforts. A farmer lent us a horse to fetch it. We had about five miles to go. Then at the village we borrowed another horse, and, with the help of about half a dozen of the squad, and the village women and children cheering us as we

43

sweated, we pulled, pushed and shoved the brokendown caravan right to the top of the Downs. That job took hours. . . .'

The Germans immediately stigmatized the LDV as *'francs-tireurs'*, outside the protection afforded by international law. However, in June 1940 enthusiastic but untrained Volunteers were more of a menace to their fellow-citizens than the enemy. The roadblock became a new and potentially lethal hazard for motorists to negotiate. A schoolmaster, J. H. Leakey, recalled an unnerving encounter:

> 'I remember one night being called over about 1 a.m. to visit the little boys at Benenden as one of them was rather ill. I climbed into the car cursing at the thought of a three-mile drive through the middle of the night. As I was turning down Golford corner an uncouth youth, flourishing some sort of musket of ancient vintage, held me up. As he seemed extremely uncertain how to manipulate his weapon he filled me with an agony of apprehension. "For God's sake, put that bloody thing down," I said. "I am sure that you will do either yourself or me severe damage if you are not careful." He meekly obliged and laid the musket to the ground. He then asked to see my papers, and bent over unarmed, reading them by the light of my side lamps. Then, having given me back my papers, he picked up his blunderbuss and allowed me to go, obviously feeling very pleased with himself over the whole affair.'

In the late summer and autumn of 1940 there was a series of invasion scares: jumpy Home Guard lookouts mistook the puffs of anti-aircraft shells for descending parachutists, or the anti-glider stakes glistening on a deserted moonlit beach for the massed ranks of a seaborne invasion force. One unit guarding the coast in Glamorgan took a more sanguine view of how to deal with the invaders. Among their number was a sixty-three-year-old Zulu, a former circus lion tamer who had settled in Wales. It was confidently expected that his appearance on the shoreline as the invasion barges hove into view would convince the Germans that they had made a serious error in navigation.

Inevitably the Home Guard's engagingly amateurish approach was forced to submit to more orthodox military disciplines. At the beginning of August 1940 its units were affiliated to county regiments and the process of integration with the Army begun. In February 1941 a formal system of ranks was introduced with commissions for officers. At the end of the year conscription brought an end to the purely voluntary nature of the Home Guard.

With the introduction of army disciplines came army bureaucracy. Commanders were buried under an avalanche of red tape; perhaps the most bizarre example, issued in the spring of 1942, was a set of detailed instructions on the correct procedures to be observed when burying Mohammedan members of the Home Guard.

In the summer of 1940 training had largely been left to the individual initiative of local commanders. The most notable freelance effort was the training school at Osterley Park run by Tom Wintringham, a former Communist who had commanded the International Brigade's British contingent in the Spanish Civil War. Wintringham was a passionate advocate of guerrilla warfare, and his star turn at Osterley was a trio of Spanish miners who taught Volunteers how to destroy tanks. Five thousand men, including some from regular army units, passed through Wintringham's school between July and October 1940, after which it became 'War Office No. 1 School' for the Home Guard. Eventually four War Office schools were established, from which 'travelling wings' were dispatched to train units all over the country.

In spite of the excellent new training programme, the Home Guard was still capable of reducing the most serious manoeuvres to surreal slapstick. On Whit Sunday 1941 Home Guard units assembled in the village of Loudwater to stage an ambitious demonstration of their skill in building and manning tank traps. Nothing was left to chance. Working back from the roadblock, it was carefully calculated exactly where each 'tank' in the enemy column would grind to a halt:

These spots thus definitely located and suitably marked, the position for each Home Guard ambush party could then be chosen and they, concealed behind the garden wall, . . . merely had to plaster their own particular tank with Molotov cocktails, sticky or anti-tank bombs and flame-throwers, and then shoot up the crews when they emerged from the tanks, as they grew too hot to hold them.

It could, therefore, readily be seen that, provided the Hun played the game and stuck to the rules, the destruction of all the tanks in the trap was . . . a piece of cake. . . . Tanks as a rule were represented by private cars, Molotov cocktails and sticky bombs by small bags of soot or chalk (which burst on impact with devastating results), anti-tank bombs by thunderflashes or home-made bombs, and flame-throwers by stirrup pumps. . . .

The Company Commander attended the demonstration. . . . 'I reached,' he said, 'the Loudwater road junction just before 07.30 hours. It was a beautiful spring morning. . . . Shortly afterwards the first tank came round the bend and obediently halted on seeing the obstruction. A shower of Molotov cocktails, hurled from behind the bushes of the nearest garden, immediately struck it with unerring precision and we then waited for the anti-tank bomb which was finally to disable it. There occurred instead, however, almost directly behind me, a terrific disturbance, a noise like that of a big rocket at a firework display.

'On turning round, I saw the most extraordinary sight; two figures standing amid the bushes of a cottage garden enveloped in a thick cloud of black smoke. One of them seemed to have lost both eyebrows and the entire half of what had been a fine crop of auburn hair, while the other had all the appearance of a jet-black nigger. . . . It soon became clear that a home-made anti-tank bomb had not been entirely successful. First aid was quickly rendered at platoon HQ. . . . For some days two of Loudwater's . . . most intrepid anti-tank fighters were most definitely out of the war.

'A move was now made to the second tank, which was waiting patiently for treatment at a spot where the right-angle turn in the road had enabled it to observe that the first tank had stopped ahead of it.

'This happened to be immediately in front of and a few yards distant from the churchyard gate, and the platoon commander informed us that the attack would be made with Molotov cocktails and a flame-thrower, concealed behind a brick wall of the Vicarage garden, at right angles to the church. On the signal being given the tank was quickly covered with a glorious coating of soot and chalk, followed by a vigorous jet of water from the stirrup pump deputising for the flame-thrower. There was a plentiful supply of water and the jet was striking the windscreen and cascading along and over the roof of the car in fine style. . . . If it had been the intention to synchronize this deluge of water with the opening of the church door to let the congregation out at the end of the early service, the timing could not have been more perfect and exact. I saw a group of people at the door of the church wiping the water from their clothes, and I heard them angrily declaiming that it was simply disgraceful for the Home Guard to wash their dirty cars outside the church door on Sunday mornings.'

Will Hay himself could not have contrived a scene of such chaos.

Above: The Home Guard conduct a training exercise on a bomb site in the City of London. Many of these bomb-site manoeuvres were fought with the utmost ferocity. *Right:* Although by the autumn of 1941 the Home Guard was an increasingly well-equipped and disciplined body, it is the 'Dad's Army' image which persists in the popular memory and is well illustrated by the unorthodox defensive positions taken up by members of this Home Guard platoon during an 'invasion' exercise.

Left: Chaos reigns in a Scottish Home Guard exercise as local units tangle with their own version of one of the great bogeymen of the early war years, the German parachutist fiendishly disguised in tweedy female attire and doubtless concealing a bomb in the pram.
Below: 'Fifth Columnists' are arrested by a Home Guard platoon led by an officer who bears more than a passing resemblance to Arthur Lowe's Captain Mannering.

Left: A review of the small craft used by the Home Guard to patrol Britain's rivers and waterways.

Opposite, top: An exercise in camouflage. In the summer of 1940 a network of about 20 Home Guard 'Auxiliary Units' was formed to fight on as 'stay behind' resistance groups if Britain fell. They were to operate from secret dumps and well-stocked underground hide-outs. The basic unit comprised one officer in command of a 'striking force' of 12 men commanded by a subaltern; later two signallers were added. These units were to be supplemented by small 'cells' composed of members of the Home Guard, selected for their resourcefulness, knowledge of the country and skill in fieldcraft. They were trained in sabotage and the use of high-explosives. Had they been put to the test, it is doubtful whether these guerrilla units could have achieved much, and their activities might well have provoked savage reprisals against the civilian population. *Opposite, bottom:* A section leader gives instructions to a mounted Home Guard patrol.

In the summer of 1943 there were 1100 Home Guard battalions, a total of 1.75 million men. The influx of teenagers from early in 1942 had reduced the average age to under thirty, and the proportion of 'old sweats' had dwindled to 7 per cent. The Home Guards' dress and weaponry were now almost identical to that of the regular Army, although a knowledgeable observer like John Brophy could always spot the tell-tale differences at a parade. 'Rank after rank would march by, heads high, legs and arms swinging in easy rhythm, rifles correctly sloped, indistinguishable from regular battalions. . . . But sooner or later the eye would be caught by a pair of sloping shoulders, or a distended waistline, an arm or a leg which, half pathetically, half absurdly, could never for long merge into the corporate rhythm.' Corporal Jones was alive and well and still doing his bit in the Home Guard.

Three years after the formation of the LDV the Home Guard retained the remarkable diversity which had marked the heady days of the Volunteers. In the remote Scottish Highlands units conducted Maquis-like manoeuvres which recalled the campaigns of Montrose; short, savage close-quarter encounters on bomb sites characterized the exercises undertaken by Home Guards in the big cities; the Cobble Hall platoon trained on an assault course and bomb-practice range prepared by the golf course's greenkeeper and his staff. Home Guard patrols criss-crossed Lake Windermere in motor launches, rode ponies over the Welsh hills and hunters over the Devon moors. The House of Commons Home Guard housed their Northover projector, a highly unreliable anti-tank weapon, in the Speaker's dining room. The BBC had its own unit in which, to the great amusement of the newsreader Wilfred Pickles, the Corporation's senior executives were ordered about by the Broadcasting House commissionaires, old soldiers to a man.

The Home Guard was never put to the ultimate test against the German Army. At the time of greatest danger, in the summer of 1940, its effectiveness would have been very limited. Although it comprised a million men under arms, its static nature meant that only those units in the Southeast – where the invasion would have come – could have rendered any immediate assistance to the Army. But the amount of men and arms available at any given moment was a problem which would have taxed the most resourceful military mind. One afternoon that summer a parachute landing was reported in Croydon. At the disposal of the local platoon commander was just one man – the rest were about their business in London. By the end of the day he had assembled a force of fifteen men whose armament consisted of one rifle, ten cartridges, a revolver and a shotgun.

However, at this time of national peril it was the Home Guard's very lack of mobility which proved an invaluable asset. The regular Army was in desperate need of training, but this could not be achieved if it was committed to the defence of Britain's coastline, factories, public utilities, airfields and thousands of 'vulnerable points' (VPs). The Home Guard's availability for these duties released thousands of troops for training and relieved the Army of a strain which might have proved intolerable. By the end of June the Southern Railway's LDV units alone were patrolling at nearly 500 VPs in its system, four times as many as those guarded by the Army.

From 1942 the Home Guard also provided valuable training for sixteen- and seventeen-year-olds who entered its ranks before their call-up. The Home Guard also served as a back-up to the Civil Defence services and the anti-aircraft arm. By September 1944 nearly 150,000 Home Guard men were serving in AA batteries.

On a social rather than a military level, Home Guard duties, however taxing after a day's work, provided much-needed companionship for men whose families had been evacuated. In the urban areas the Home Guard was a focus for a wide-range of social activities, from football matches to whist drives.

The Home Guard was a uniquely British institution, full of historical resonances. In its early days, Sir John Falstaff and his motley crew of camp followers – Nym, Bardolph and Pistol – might have made themselves at home in its ranks. For all their lack of soldierly qualities, they would have been familiar with the pikes issued in 1941. But two years later they would have given way to the well-equipped force which took its place on manoeuvres alongside regular units. Its men were truly members of a People's Army in a People's War.

The Home Guard stood down at the end of November 1944. Throughout Britain there were parades to mark the occasion. Henry Smith, a member of the Ministry of Food Home Guard at Colwyn Bay, has left an evocative description of his unit's standing down ceremony, which in characteristic British fashion was conducted in the driving rain:

> We stood in our hollow square in the wind and rain and saw Colonel Shennan go through the motions of making a speech. We could not hear what he said but we knew what he was saying. Then Colonel Llewellin presented the battalion flag to Maclean (the battalion commander). We cheered, as self-consciously and unconvincingly as Englishmen always cheer, except at a football match. Maclean said something; we could not hear what it was, but we knew from experience that he was giving the flag away. He always gave things away. We learned next day that he was giving it away to the Imperial War Museum. . . .
> The rain came down harder and harder and the wind rose in intensity. Colonel Llewellin loomed through the driving mist and sleet, becoming more undistinguishable from [the mountain of] Carreold Llewellin every

moment. He concluded his speech. Again we went through the motions of cheering. Colonel Llewellin gave the order, for the last time, 'Home Guards and Auxiliaries dismiss!' Symbolically, the regular rigid lines broke and dissolved into a horde of individuals seeking shelter from the storm. As we turned away, it was difficult to get any clear picture of what most of us were feeling. For four years now we had given up a very large proportion of the time not claimed by the Ministry to our military training. Now we could do in our spare time all the things we had wanted to do. Instead of lying behind hedges with rifles in the foothills, we could climb the mountains. Instead of reading War Office manuals, we could read real books, and establish again that contact with things of the mind and the spirit on which we had turned our backs for so long. Or could we? Was there not a barrier between us and our peacetime activities and interests which would remain there all the time that our younger brothers-in-arms were laying down their lives on the battlefield? Would not the resumption of the peacetime habit of life constitute the re-erection of that barrier between them and us which had almost vanished during our years of service? We did not know. The show was over. It was still raining.

In London the standing down of the Home Guard was marked by a showbusiness tribute organized by the *Daily Mail* and staged at the Albert Hall. Vera Lynn was one of the many stars who, in a memorable evening, paid tribute to the Home Guard. The *Daily Mail*'s review of the show captures perfectly the atmosphere of the last months of the war:

From all directions, Home Guards came to pack the hall. They besieged the doors. By their own transport, by buses, by taxis, and on foot, they filled the roads leading to the great circular building. From the blackout – even

Vera Lynn in the spotlight at one of the many concerts held in the Albert Hall in honour of those who served in the war.

the dim-out was black – they plunged into a haze of blinding light. From the silence of the London streets they plunged into a blare of sound. Louis Levy and his band 'played them in'. My own seat was in the First Circle. I looked down upon a sea of khaki. Here and there it was broken by islands of colour – the scattered womenfolk of the Home Guard. As turn succeeded turn on the programme, each announced by Leslie Mitchell, the tension in the audience perceptibly grew. Bennett and Williams fired their machine-gun jokes – one of them crowning his khaki uniform with an opera hat. The first joke created a ripple, the third a wave, the sixth a hurricane of laughter. There was no 'stickiness' in last night's audience. They came with the intention of having a good time, with the expectation of having a good time and a good time they had, in full measure, pressed down and running over. After Bennett and Williams came 'The Waters of England' – the immortal Gert and Daisy. One phrase of theirs caught the imagination of the whole audience: 'The blokes in Burma aren't half proud of their fathers.' Rob Wilton, the caricature of all the caricatured Home Guards in all the Home Guard jokes of all time, received a great hand. Suddenly the lights dimmed. In the two or three lines focused on the stage the smoke from a thousand pipes, from three thousand cigarettes and cigars eddied and swirled. Into the blaze of light came a slim figure in a billowing powder-blue gown – the Sweetheart of the Forces, Vera Lynn. As she sang, silence came to the Albert Hall; a hush through which the true voice soared. It rang clear, an English voice. . . . In the dimness, for the first time, one could appreciate the age of the Home Guard. Bald heads gleamed, silver heads shone, grey heads glowed. Here was the army of the middle-aged. But the old youth came back to the middle-aged when George Robey and Vi Loraine re-created, towards the end of this war, the furore they created throughout the last. . . . Highest light of a night of high lights was Cicely Courtneidge. First she sang a repertory of her old choruses, then suddenly the tempo changed, and with it the temper of the audience, in a brilliant monologue. With superbly scored incidental music, she gave the 'Stand Down, Gentlemen' – a piece of irregular verse recalling the darkest of our dark days and our triumph over them. The beating of the hands was like the whirring of thousands of wings as a multitude of birds was disturbed. The applause even destroyed the fortissimo of the amplified band. In the corridors at half time, over cups of tea, in a hundred accents, in a thousand phrases, one sentiment was uttered – 'Jolly good show!'

52

4

THE BATTLE OF BRITAIN

The high summer of 1940 was well nigh perfect: in July and August England basked in warm sunshine under cloudless blue skies, the kind of idyllic summer which seems to have vanished for ever. But the benign skies were flecked with vapour trails which betrayed the urgency of the times. For it was here, 20,000 ft above our countryside and cities, that the fate of the nation hung in the balance.

After the fall of France and the evacuation of the British Expeditionary Force, mainland Britain remained as Hitler's obvious target. But the Führer had neither anticipated this nor made any plans to deal with it. He had assumed that, once France had been knocked out of the war, Britain would seek peace terms. Hitler ardently desired peace with Britain. This would provide him with a buffer against the United States and release his armies for his cherished objective, the invasion of the Soviet Union.

At first he decided to wait until the nerve of the British cracked, as it had at Munich in 1938. He told General Jodl, 'The British have lost the war, but they don't know it; one must give them time, and they will come round.'

The British did not come round. On 27 May, before the Dunkirk evacuation had begun, the British Cabinet had considered the possibility of peace negotiations, with Mussolini acting as an intermediary, an idea whose chief supporters were yesterday's men, Chamberlain and the Foreign Secretary Lord Halifax. The next day Winston Churchill asserted his authority. At a meeting attended by all ministers of Cabinet rank he announced, 'Whatever happens at Dunkirk, we shall fight on.' There was spontaneous applause and shouts of 'Well done, Prime Minister!' Churchill and his generals began at once to prepare to meet a German invasion. When it would come they could not tell; that it would come seemed certain.

Hitler's bluff had been called, and he turned to plans for an invasion of southeast England on a front from Deal to Brighton, eventually set for 17 September. This was not a prospect which pleased the German Navy, which had not recovered from the losses it had suffered in Norway. The German Army remained optimistic; its C-in-C, General von Brauchitsch, even went so far as to boast that the operation, code-named Sealion, would be little more than 'a large-scale river crossing'. Hitler wavered, sharing the misgivings of the Navy's C-in-C, Grand-Admiral Raeder. He concluded that the invasion should be undertaken only as a last resort, a mopping-up operation after the enemy had already been broken by blockade and air attack. Sealion was never conceived as a major offensive, launched simultaneously by all three arms, in which the Luftwaffe would have joined battle with the RAF over the Channel and the landing beaches immediately before and during the landings – a strategy which might well have overwhelmed the British defences. Hitler shrank from the risk; anything less than total victory would have dealt a blow to his prestige. Air supremacy over the Channel and southeast England was to be secured before the invasion went ahead. In the meantime the invasion barges began to mass in the Channel ports.

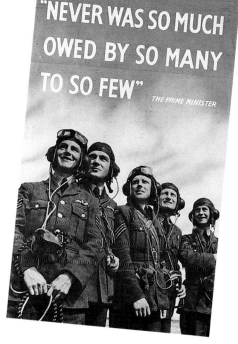

"NEVER WAS SO MUCH OWED BY SO MANY TO SO FEW" THE PRIME MINISTER

53

A squadron of Hurricanes in flight. Although less glamorous than the legendary Spitfire, the rugged Hurricane bore the brunt of the fighting in the Battle of Britain (July–November 1940). The top-scoring Fighter Command squadron of the Battle of Britain, No. 303, flew Hurricanes, and is credited with 126½ confirmed victories.

Throughout these deliberations one man was oozing confidence. The C-in-C of the Luftwaffe, Reichsmarshal Hermann Goering, believed that a mere four days would be sufficient to eliminate the RAF south of a line from Chelmsford to Gloucester. After the easy triumphs in Poland and France, Goering was convinced that the British could be brought to their knees by air power alone.

At his disposal were three air fleets: the largest, Luftflotte 2, was based in northern France, Belgium and Holland; Luftflotte 3 was based in northwest France; and the smaller Luftflotte 5 was based in Norway and Denmark. Together these air fleets could muster some 3500 aircraft. With 75 per cent serviceability, Goering could count on approximately 1000 twin-engined bombers, 250 Ju 87 'Stuka' dive-bombers and 1000 single-engined Me109 and twin-engined Me110 escort fighters to throw against the 700 aircraft of Air Chief Marshal Sir Hugh Dowding's Fighter Command – two thirds of them Hawker Hurricanes – which were immediately available for operations.

In the coming battle Fighter Command enjoyed several significant advantages over the enemy. First, the 'Chain Home' system of fifty early-warning radar stations established on the coastline from Land's End to Scotland. Secondly, the intelligence gathered from 'Ultra', the top-secret device which had broken German codes, and the radio-listening 'Y' service; this was used to build up a reasonably accurate picture of the Luftwaffe's order of battle. Thirdly, the benefits derived from engaging the enemy over home territory, where pilots could fly more sorties and stood a good chance of living to fight another day if they were shot down.

Fighter Command's front-line aircraft were the Hawker Hurricane and the Supermarine Spitfire. The Hurricane, the world's first eight-gun monoplane fighter, was now edging towards obsolescence. It could not compete with the Me109 in speed and rate of climb, but it was a steady gun platform, easy to fly, capable of absorbing a huge amount of punishment and, with its fabric covering, easy to repair; it was to bear the brunt of the fighting in the Battle of Britain. The Spitfire, the most famous aircraft ever in service with the RAF, could out-turn the Me109 in a dogfight but frequently could not follow its German opponent down in the classic fighter manoeuvre of a half roll and dive; the Me109's direct-injection engine kept on running under negative gravity, whereas the Spitfire's Merlin, with a float-chamber carburettor, tended to cut out.

Seemingly invincible, the Luftwaffe entered the battle labouring under a number of serious disadvantages, not all of them immediately grasped at the time. By the end of the Battle of France the Luftwaffe had suffered heavy overall losses and needed time to rest and regroup. On the eve of the Battle of Britain deliveries of aircraft were actually slowing down. During the same period British fighter production plans were exceeded by 40 per cent.

Conceived and equipped as a close-support instrument of Blitzkrieg warfare, the Luftwaffe was about to launch a strategic offensive for which it had not been designed. Its high command had seriously under-estimated the vulnerability in daylight operations of its twin-engined bombers and their sluggish Me110 escorts. The Stuka, which had acquired a terrifying reputation in Poland and France, proved to be a sitting duck when pulling out at the bottom of its dive. The Me109 was a superb air-superiority weapon when operating over advancing armour, but its short range limited it to a maximum of 30 minutes over Britain, and even this was eaten away at combat settings.

In the first phase of the battle the Luftwaffe made a series of probing attacks on coastal targets and convoys, seeking to lure Fighter Command squadrons over the Channel and into a fight in which they would be cut up by superior numbers. They frequently flew fighter sweeps in the vicinity of the raiding force. These the RAF learned to ignore, provided they could be recognized in time.

It was during this period of deadly sparring, on 10 July, that a BBC reporter, Charles Gardner, gave a famous impromptu live commentary on a dogfight over 'Hellfire Corner' at the tip of Kent: 'There's one coming down in flames – there somebody's hit a German – and he's coming down – there's a long streak – he's coming down completely out of control – a long streak of smoke – ah, the man's baled out by parachute – the pilot's baled out by parachute – he's a Junkers 87 [a Stuka] and he's going slap into the sea and there he goes – sma-a-ash. Oh boy, I've never seen anything so good as this – the RAF fighters have really got these boys taped!'

Hitler still nursed hopes of a British surrender. On 19 July, addressing the Reichstag, he appealed to the British Empire, 'which it was never my intention to destroy or even to harm. . . . I consider myself in a position to make this appeal since I am not the vanquished begging favours, but the victor speaking in the name of reason.' Within an hour the BBC had broadcast a curt rejection of these grandiloquent overtures.

The battle now slipped into a higher gear. On 30 July Hitler ordered Goering to prepare 'immediately and with greatest haste . . . the great battle of the German Air Force against England.' On the morning of 2 August the puzzled citizens of Hampshire and Somerset received thousands of air-dropped leaflets which contained the text of Hitler's speech under the heading 'The Last Appeal to Reason'. (Having been gathered up, they were put to good use, in auctions for the Red Cross.) Later on 2 August Goering was issued with the final orders for *Adlertag* (Eagle Day) on which the destruction of Fighter Command was to be accomplished.

Adlertag was set for 10 August, but bad weather caused its postponement for three days. Nevertheless, the fighting increased in intensity. German bombers carried out extensive minelaying operations in the Thames and Humber estuaries and the dock approaches of Penzance, Plymouth, Liverpool, Southampton, Falmouth and Belfast. On 12 August a heavy attack was made on the Portsmouth docks. Fifteen of the German bombers were diverted to attack the radar station at Ventnor, whose tall latticed masts offered conspicuous targets. The Ventnor station was put out of action until 23 August, but those at Dover, Rye and Pevensey – which also came under attack – were quickly working again using their 'Buried Reserve'. Ventnor's disappearance from the chain was effectively camouflaged by the remaining stations, and to the listening German radio intelligence officers there appeared to be no appreciable reduction in the 'Chain Home' network's efficiency. Fatally, the Luftwaffe chose not to press home its attacks on the radar stations. On 15 August Goering, presiding over a meeting of his three air fleet commanders, had concluded, 'It is doubtful whether there is any point in continuing the attacks on the radar stations in view of the fact that not one of those attacked has so far been out of operation.'

From 13 August the Luftwaffe concentrated its attention on Fighter Command bases, particularly the seven key sector stations – Biggin Hill, Debden, Hornchurch, Kenley, Northolt, North Weald and Tangmere. Then, on 15 August, all three air fleets combined to throw five successive

Opposite: Children crouched in a slit trench in Kent watch the dogfights raging over what became known as 'Hellfire Corner'.

waves against targets as far apart as Portland in the southwest and Tyneside in the northeast. In what became known as 'Black Thursday' the Germans suffered overall losses of seventy-two aircraft – twice those of the RAF – and the badly mauled Luftflotte 5 was withdrawn from the battle. On the same day Goering issued instructions that no aircrew operating over England should contain more than one officer.

For the inhabitants of the Home Counties the battle raging over their heads had an almost abstract quality, traced in the twisting vapour trails in the sky. Sometimes faint bursts of machine-gun fire reached their ears; and sometimes a shower of empty shell cases came clattering to earth to be scooped up by a rush of children.

At regular intervals a member of the Luftwaffe put in a surprise appearance. One such incident, in Kent, was recalled by Hubert S. Banner:

The red-letter days were, of course, those when the exchanges overhead produced visible results in the form of Nazi airmen floating to earth. First you would discern a white speck against the blue, apparently stationary. But the speck would grow larger until you could make out its umbrella-top shape, and then at last you would be able to see the minute figure dangling beneath. And what a rush there would be in the direction of the spot where the figure seemed likely to descend. Sometimes there was more than one. On one memorable occasion I saw five on their way down simultaneously, and the difficulty then was to decide in which of the five directions to rush. . . .

I saw my first Nazi at close quarters during those memorable days. My wife and I had just finished lunch when we were startled by a 'zoom' that ended in a loud crash. Rushing to the window, we saw a column of black smoke rising above the treetops, and a few moments later began a crackling fusillade that reminded one of the Fifth of November. Machine-gun ammunition popping off in the bonfire, I decided. We jumped into the car and drove towards the smoke and noise, and soon we were overtaking a throng of cyclists and pedestrians all heading in the same direction.

The scene of the crash was on a golf course. and a good-sized crowd had arrived there before us. . . . The German fighter-bomber had hit the tree tops on its descent, and there it lay, sprawling broken-backed on the greensward. . . . It was consuming rapidly in its own flames, and the empty cartridge cases leaped out of the pyre in all directions. The police had formed a cordon. Sternly, they ordered the mob to keep its distance, but the small boys were too much for them. They dived and ducked through the cordon singly and in dozens, cheerfully contemptuous of the awful penalties attached to interfering with captured enemy property. . . .

Beneath the trees . . . lay the Nazi airman. A first-aid party was in attendance. Tender hands were bandaging his cut forehead and broken leg. He was silent now, but I learned afterwards that when first dragged from his burning plane he had made noise enough until one of the men said to him, 'Be a man and shut up, can't you? You asked for it, and now you've got it.' Not another squeak had come from him after that rebuke.

Meanwhile the police were examining his effects. . . . They drew forth in turn a carton of Californian dried raisins, a large slab of Cadbury's chocolate, and – crowning insult – a packet of twenty Gold Flake. Many of the men who had thus far kept silence could no longer restrain their feelings when they caught sight of those Gold Flakes. They might be able to forgive the German for having come over with the intention of blowing them to bits, but not for having brought with him cigarettes looted from our abandoned stores in France.

After a lull caused by poor weather the battle reached another crisis on 30 August when Biggin Hill received the first of six major attacks which

destroyed most of its buildings. Working vital equipment in the open, and transferring the operations room to a local butcher's shop, the airfield defied all attempts to knock it out. On 4 September so many raids were being plotted at Bentley Priory, Fighter Command HQ, that the operations table was swamped.

The RAF's loss of fighters in the air and on the ground were now outstripping the supply of new aircraft. Over the ten days between 8 and 18 August the RAF downed 367 enemy aircraft for losses of 213 (of which thirty had been destroyed on the ground); but fewer than 150 new Hurricanes and Spitfires were supplied during this period. There was also a growing shortage of experienced pilots. Over the same ten-day period Fighter Command lost 154 pilots killed, missing or badly wounded, while only sixty-three novices joined the squadrons from the training units. By the opening week of September Dowding's squadrons had, on average, only sixteen operational pilots out of their full complement of twenty-six. By the end of the week there were no fresh squadrons to replace the battered units in the Southeast. The remorseless statistics of attrition had revealed the ever-widening gap between casualties and replacements, both in hardware and human beings. As Churchill wrote later, 'The scales had tipped against Fighter Command. There was much anxiety.'

The Luftwaffe too was finding it hard to make up the losses in men and materiel. Of the 1000 aircraft it dispatched across the Channel every day, only about 25 per cent were bombers. To protect them, the Me109s were pulled in tight above, ahead and on the flanks of their formations, further reducing the combat efficiency of the fighters.

At this point, with Fighter Command reeling on the ropes, German strategy took a new turn. Late in the afternoon of 7 September the Luftwaffe launched its first daylight raid on London, ordered by Hitler in retaliation against the Bomber Command raid on Berlin on the night of 25–26 August. The Blitz on Britain's cities had begun. That night the Chiefs of Staff issued the codeword 'Cromwell', putting the Home Forces on full alert. Many commanders mistakenly believed that an invasion was in progress. Church bells were rung by the Home Guard; in some places army units demolished bridges; through the night citizen and regular soldiers kept a tense watch.

'Cromwell' was withdrawn on 19 September, four days after the climax of the Battle of Britain. German intelligence – consistently over-optimistic – had estimated that Fighter Command had only 100 aircraft left. But on 15 September the Luftwaffe suffered a crushing reverse when two heavily escorted waves of bombers ran into nearly 300 British fighters over London. Overall German losses were fifty-five, and of the remaining aircraft at least a quarter were heavily battle-damaged. Fighter Command lost twenty-eight aircraft, and, in one of the exultant bursts of overclaiming which were a feature of the battle, claimed 185 enemy shot down. Air superiority had been decisively denied to the Luftwaffe, and on 12 October Hitler ordered the indefinite postponement of Sealion.

The last major daylight raids occurred on 30 September, the Luftwaffe losing forty-one aircraft in attacks on London and the West Country town of Yeovil. During the autumn the bombers were to return by night.

On 20 August, at the height of the battle, Winston Churchill made a speech in the House of Commons in which he declared, 'Never in the field of human conflict was so much owed by so many to so few.' The story goes that one young fighter pilot's response was the laconic observation

Vapour trails in the blue summer sky over St Paul's Cathedral paint an abstract picture of the desperate fight for survival in August 1940.

that the Prime Minister's tribute must surely refer to his squadron's mess bills.

The aircrew of the RAF had long enjoyed a reputation for insouciant individualism, but the realities of the Battle of Britain were far grimmer than the subsequent myths of devil-may-care knights of the sky, downing their Gin and Its and exchanging ironic banter before scrambling to meet the enemy. In combat they went into the mincing machine, flying as many as six or seven sorties a day. Often they took off wounded, nearly always exhausted. A fully trained squadron could be chewed up in as little as ten days. One pilot recalled, 'We were dead. We were too tired even to get drunk. You simply never saw a pilot drunk.' Another, Colin Gray, spoke for many when he recalled, 'It was no picnic despite what anyone might say later. . . . Most of us were pretty scared all the bloody time; you only felt happy when the battle was over and you were on your way home. Then you felt safe, for a bit, anyway.'

Ironically, the RAF had entered the battle with its reputation at a low ebb. 'Where was the RAF?' was the bitter complaint of many of those

who had been evacuated from Dunkirk and who felt that they had not been given sufficient air cover. Earlier, in the Battle of France, Air Chief Marshal Dowding had resisted intense pressure to feed more of his squadrons into what was clearly a doomed cause. His determination to husband his slender resources ensured that the RAF entered the Battle of Britain with the narrowest of margins over the enemy. Even today the remote, austere Dowding, nicknamed 'Stuffy' by his subordinates, has not received the recognition which is his due.

His fighter pilots were an elite, at the cutting edge of the battle. Behind them was a complex of auxiliary services which kept their Hurricanes and Spitfires in the air. The battle could not have been won without the ground crews, the women of the WAAF and the men of the Royal Observer Corps. The civilians of the Post Office War Group maintained communications between radar stations, observer posts and the RAF's operations rooms and headquarters. The Civilian Repair Organization, a remarkable alliance of garages, car dealers, warehouses and small contractors, patched up hundreds of damaged aircraft; by mid-July it was restoring 160 aircraft a week to operational usefulness. The men of No. 1 Civilian Repair Unit at Oxford worked a fourteen-hour day seven days a week, and pilots were known to fly damaged aircraft straight to Oxford for first aid.

Civilians from Oxford's Morris motor works provided the majority of personnel in the RAF's No. 50 Maintenance Unit, cannibalizing wrecked aircraft for vital spare parts. Their depot eventually covered over 100 acres of Oxfordshire countryside, a sprawling warplane graveyard which looked 'not so much like a cemetery as a wartime mushroom town; a City of Wreckage where the oblong piles of debris were fantastic houses, and the wing tips poking their way out from irregular roofs were the crazy smokeless chimneys.'

Over the din of battle came the irrepressible, gruff voice of Lord Beaverbrook, the Minister of Aircraft Production, who on 10 July made this stirring appeal:

'Women of Britain, give us your aluminium. We want it and we want it now. . . . We will turn your pots and pans into Spitfires and Hurricanes, Blenheims and Wellingtons. I ask therefore that everyone who has pots and pans, kettles and vacuum cleaners, hat pegs, coat-hangers, shoe-trees, bathroom fittings and household ornaments, cigarette boxes or any other articles made wholly or partly of aluminium, should hand them in at once to the local headquarters of the Women's Voluntary Service.'

This produced a flood of ironmongery but only a trickle of high-grade aluminium. More successful was the Spitfire Fund, which encouraged individuals, groups and whole communities to 'buy' an aircraft. Quite arbitrarily a Spitfire was priced at £5000 and a bomber at £20,000. Sadly, only a few donors chose to buy the doughty but unglamorous Hurricane. You could check your progress against a price list – sixpence for a rivet, 15 shillings for the blast tube of a machine gun, £22 for a small bomb, and £2000 for a wing. By the spring of 1941 over £13 million had been raised by the Spitfire Fund. The threat of invasion was now receding. Victory had been secured by the few, and the many.

Opposite, top: Some of 'The Few' – pilots of No. 602 Squadron, Fighter Command's highest-scoring Spitfire squadron in the Battle of Britain, with 102 confirmed victories. *Opposite, bottom:* The great aluminium drive, dreamt up by Lord Beaverbrook, which achieved limited results. *Above:* Workmen removing railings in August 1940, a scheme launched with the initial aim of collecting half a million tons of scrap, enough to build 300 destroyers. Some of the raids on railings led to accusations of 'sabotage' and 'vandalism'. By September 1944 the total weight of railings demolished had reached a million tons, much of which never got farther than the huge rusting piles on to which it was dumped.

5

THE BLITZ

The Blitz thrust us all into the front line. Far from destroying us, as Hitler intended, it brought the nation together. The evidence was all around, most strikingly in the way in which the bombing broke down the traditional barriers of British reserve. Shared danger produced the novel sight of people talking to each other without being introduced!

When you were in a shelter at the height of a raid, class differences didn't matter. Nor did they count for much among those who fought to keep London working, in the thick of the worst that the Luftwaffe could throw at us: the air-raid warden poking his head around the door of a shelter to ask if everybody was all right; the rescue workers searching desperately in the ruins of shattered homes for the signs of remaining life; the fire-watchers standing guard in empty buildings; the boys in the Fire Brigade, who risked their lives nearly every night; the women of the WVS, whose mobile canteens provided hot meals and, above all, comfort for families who had been bombed out in the raids. The interlocking activities of all these groups bred a tremendous feeling of camaraderie which lasted throughout the war. People depended on each other in a way which would have seemed unimaginable in peacetime.

Everyone had their own 'bomb story', often embroidered and dramatized in the retelling but a genuine reflection of the ordeal we all lived through and our determination to show the Nazis that 'London can take it'. The bombing was the backdrop to all our lives: the row of houses in the next street flattened by a parachute mine; nights spent in the Anderson shelter; the wail of the all-clear siren. Late one night I drove home to Barking from a show through a combination of blackout and London 'pea-souper' which slowed my little Austin to a stuttering crawl. The warning siren sounded as I inched my way through Poplar, which had taken a terrific pasting since the beginning of the Blitz and was popularly known as 'Bomb Alley'. On went my tin hat, a precaution against any shrapnel which might tear through the canvas hood of the little car. I continued to roll through the fog, isolated from the rest of the world, with the sounds of the Blitz all around me: the drone of the enemy aircraft overhead; the 'whang-whang' of a nearby ack-ack battery; the crump of bombs, all of which seemed to be aimed at me. I finally reached home unscathed but exhausted.

I also have vivid memories of inspecting a huge parachute mine which had crashed through the roof of the Palladium but had failed to explode. When I arrived it had been safely defused but was still hanging in the wings of the theatre like a sinister stage prop. I cut off a piece of the flapping 'chute as a souvenir. It seemed strange to come away with so soft a reminder of so terrible a weapon crammed into my bag.

That parachute mine gave me a rare night off. After the initial shock of the Blitz it was 'business as usual', whether you were singing at the Palladium or running the corner shop. Perhaps more than at any other

time in our recent history the nine months of the Blitz demonstrated the strength, good humour and courage of ordinary Britons who found themselves in extraordinary circumstances.

In his first War Directive, issued on 21 August 1939, Adolf Hitler informed his Chiefs of Staff, 'The decision regarding attacks on London is reserved to me.' But the Führer was pre-empted by a number of Luftwaffe aircrew lost in the night skies over England. On the night of 24–25 August several Me111 bombers missed their targets around the River Medway and jettisoned their bombs over the East End of London.

On the following night the RAF retaliated: eighty-one bombers raided Berlin for the first time, returning on subsequent nights. On 4 September Hitler made a broadcast speech from the German capital in which he threatened to raze British towns and cities. In that familiar rasping voice he told his audience, 'The British drop bombs . . . on civilian residential quarters and farms and villages. . . . I did not reply because I believed that they would stop. Mr Churchill took this as a sign of weakness. The

British will know that we are giving our answer. We shall stop the handiwork of those night pirates, so help us God.' Three days later Reichsmarshal Hermann Goering was given permission to attack London.

On Saturday, 7 September, Londoners awoke to a brilliant early autumn day. There was barely a wisp of cloud in the pale blue sky. Across the Channel, near Cap Gris Nez, Goering's special train, complete with its elaborate kitchen car and chef, was drawn up in a siding. The Reichsmarshal had decided personally to direct what he confidently expected to be the last phase in the Battle of Britain.

That afternoon Goering stood on the cliffs at Cap Gris Nez, surrounded by an entourage of high-ranking Luftwaffe officers, war correspondents and cameramen. He was resplendent in immaculate uniform, the strap of his white-topped service cap disappearing in the folds of his chin. His binoculars swept the English coast through the warm haze. Above, the first flight of 625 bombers and 650 fighters thundered over the 22-mile stretch of water between Cap Gris Nez and Dover, en route for London.

At 4.43 in central London the sirens set up their wail and the population made for the shelters. Barbara Nixon, an air-raid warden, later wrote:

'The women were frankly fussed and ran, grabbing their children by bits of shirt or jacket; one woman rushed down, her hair a pile of soapsuds straight from the Saturday afternoon shampoo; the children were excited; the men made a point of swaggering in front of their womenfolk, and walked slowly and soberly. But nobody was seriously frightened. There had been repeated alerts and a few actual bombs dropped during the preceding weeks. Something might possibly happen this time, but probably not.

'Within a few minutes a large V-shaped formation of planes flew over us heading to the southeast. The tiny machines glinted in the sunlight and looked more like a flock of geese migrating before the winter than hostile aircraft. Soon they were followed by a smaller formation, each silver speck leaving a gossamer tail curved gracefully behind it. The old soldiers were very knowledgeable and told us that they were "ours". Later that phrase, "It's one of ours", became one of my chief superstitions, so often was it followed by the whistle and crump of bombs.

'But that afternoon the danger was still remote from us. It was the East End that was getting it. From where we were we could see the miniature silver planes circling round and round the target area in such perfect formation that they looked like a children's toy model of flying boats or chair-o-planes at a fair. It was almost impossible to imagine that they were doing damage. Occasionally there would be a few puffs of Ack-Ack, but they were too low to interrupt the rhythm of the formations. As one set of planes flew off, another V formation would fly in, stretch out in a follow-my-leader line, and circle round as its predecessor had done.

'Presently we saw a white cloud rising; it looked like a huge evening cumulus, but it grew steadily, billowing outwards and always upwards. A fire engine went by up the main road. The cloud grew to such a size that we gasped incredulously: there could not ever in history have been so gigantic a fire. Another fire engine raced by, then a third, then a fourth, clanging their bells frenziedly as they shot across the traffic lights; our local substation turned out, nearly every fire appliance in London was heading east.'

The Luftwaffe's principal targets were the London docks. The first wave of bombers dropped over 300 tons of high explosives and

thousands of incendiaries on the waterfront and the closely packed streets of West Ham, Poplar, Stepney and Bermondsey, the riverside boroughs on either side of the Thames's great double meander where the Victoria and Albert Docks, the West India Docks and the vast Surrey Commercial Docks were concentrated.

The East End had borne the brunt of the attack. Entire streets of jerry-built two-up-two-downs, thrown up cheaply by nineteenth-century speculative builders, were reduced to dust and rubble. In the docks, blazing warehouses lit the way for 250 bombers which between 8 p.m. and dawn, dropped 330 tons of high explosives and 13,000 incendiaries.

Four miles away Barbara Nixon watched the changing sky: 'As evening drew on the barrage balloons turned pink in the sunset light; or

One of the classic photographs of the war – a German He111 bomber drones over London's Isle of Dogs in September 1940.

was it the firelight? They looked pretty enough, but the enormous cloud turned an angrier red and blackened round the edges. From our vantagepoint it was remote and, from a spectacular point of view, beautiful. One had to force oneself to picture the misery and the havoc below in the most overcrowded area of London; the panic and the horror when suddenly bombs had fallen in the busy, narrow street markets and bazaars and on the rickety houses.'

After the all-clear sounded at 6.15 p.m. Barbara Nixon went to a restaurant in Soho: 'When we came out of the restaurant we stopped aghast. The whole sky to the east was blazing red. The afternoon spectacle was completely dwarfed; it seemed as though half of London must be burning, and fifty thousand firemen would not be able to put out a fire of that size. In Shaftesbury Avenue, five miles from the blaze, it was possible to read the evening paper.' Bombs were now falling on the West End.

In the East End, below a boiling pall of crimson oily smoke, firemen and the auxiliary and voluntary services fought heroically to contain the raging fires while the bombs continued to rain down. 'The whole bloody world's on fire!' said the fire officer at the Surrey Docks, where 250 acres of timber were ablaze. Before the war a 'thirty-pump' fire was considered a major incident. By midnight on 7 September there were nine fires in London rating over 100 pumps. In the Surrey Docks there were two, of 300 and 130 pumps. All nine fires were technically out of hand, unsurrounded, uncontrolled and spreading. The biggest, at Quebec Yard in the Surrey Docks, was forty times bigger than the Barbican fire of 1938, the worst blaze in London's recent history. The intense heat it generated blistered the paintwork of the fireboats trying to slip past under the lee of the opposite river bank 300 yards away. Solid embers a foot long were whirled into distant streets, starting fresh fires. Stacks of timber, drenched by the fire service, began to smoulder, dry and then burst into flames in the heat radiated from nearby blazes.

A pall of smoke hangs over the London docks on the first day of the Blitz, 7 September 1940.

For every warehouse there seemed to be a different fire. There were pepper fires, filling the firemen's lungs with stinging particles; rum fires, spilling rivers of flaming liquid into the streets; a paint fire coated the pumps with a varnish which could not be removed for weeks; a rubber fire produced billowing clouds of asphyxiating smoke. Driven from their nests, rats raced through the streets in their thousands. Blazing barges, cut loose from their wharves, floated down the river, adding to the chaos.

London's air defences were wholly ineffective. AA Command was a Cinderella service, starved of modern equipment and fully trained personnel. At the end of August 1940 the anti-aircraft strength for the whole of Britain was approximately 50 per cent of the heavy guns and 33 per cent of the light guns considered necessary in the pre-war programme. Only ninety-two heavy guns were in position in London on the first night of the Blitz, and the crews were hampered by a requirement to identify an aircraft as hostile before firing, as there were RAF night fighters operating over the capital. The fighters, relying on visual interception, were no more successful than the guns, and only a single raider was shot down that night.

For the next fifty-six nights London was to be bombed from dusk to dawn, with the intensity of the night raids being stepped up from mid-October as German bombers droned up the silver line of the Thames to the biggest target in the world. The river had created London, and now the Luftwaffe was using it as the means of the city's destruction.

In the aftermath of the raid of 7 September the authorities were confronted with a problem which they had not anticipated. Pre-war planning had been based on the expectation of huge civilian casualties in a series of short, devastating daylight raids; it was also assumed that the number of houses left standing after the bombers had gone would contain sufficient living space to house the survivors, although little thought had been given to the most efficient way of accomplishing this rehousing. But although the civilian casualties suffered in the first two nights of the Blitz were serious – amounting to nearly 1000 dead – they were but a fraction of the death toll envisaged by the planners in the 1930s. However, dealing with the dead proved easier than coping with the thousands who remained alive but homeless.

In the shock that followed the first raid, the streets of the East End were in turmoil as people whose houses had been destroyed searched for their relatives, belongings and, as night approached, some sort of shelter from the bombs. Later that day two massive evacuations began: eastwards to Epping Forest, where thousands camped out in the open, and westwards to central London, where it was believed that the shelters were deep and safe and the bombing less heavy.

Some travelled farther afield, to Reading and Oxford, where Vera Brittain was surprised to find babies' nappies hung out to dry in the seventeenth-century splendour of Christ Church's Tom quadrangle. The Oxford colleges stepped in as temporary clearing houses for these 'unauthorized evacuees'. Several hundred of them were found a home in Oxford's Majestic Cinema. Vera Brittain wrote:

> Covering the floor beneath the upturned velveteen seats of the cinema chairs, disorderly piles of mattresses, pillows, rugs and cushions indicate the 'pitches' staked out by each evacuated family. Many of the women, too dispirited to move, still lie wearily on the floor with their children beside them in the foetid air, though the hour is 11 a.m. and a warm sun is shining cheerfully on the city streets. Between the mattresses and cushions the customary collection of soiled newspapers and ancient applecores is contributing noticeably to the odoriferous atmosphere.

Above: A scene repeated in a thousand streets of the East End – clearing up after a raid. *Opposite, top:* A family tries out its stirrup pump. Designed to enable one person with a bucket of water and some sand to put out a young fire, and costing 12s 6d, it was first allocated to wardens' posts. Later many were diverted to private sale at a higher price, but there was always a shortage. As late as June 1942, 95,000 were on order, undelivered. *Opposite, bottom:* The Auxiliary Fire Service battles with a blaze in the docklands.

By the middle of September some of the worst-hit London boroughs had lost a quarter of their population. For 25,000 of the homeless who chose to stay put the only immediate relief was provided by the rough-and-ready Rest Centres, usually housed in school buildings, whose original function had been to provide accommodation for a matter of hours. At the beginning of the Blitz many homeless were stranded in them for ten days or more, often in conditions of abject squalor. The bombed-out were almost invariably caked in grime, sometimes wearing only their night clothes, but there were few rest centres with adequate washing facilities or a supply of clothes. Food was limited to bread and marge or corned beef. Frequently there was no crockery or cutlery. On 12 September a centre in Bethnal Green had only two spoons and a blunt knife. A social worker vividly recalled the Rest Centres of the early days of the Blitz: 'The picture of the rest centres in . . . those days is unforgettable. Dim figures in dejected heaps on unwashed floors in total darkness; harassed, bustling but determinedly cheerful helpers distributing eternal corned-beef sandwiches and tea – the London County Council panacea for hunger, shock, loss, misery and illness. . . . Dishevelled, half-dressed people wandering between the bombed houses and the rest centre salvaging bits and pieces, or trying to keep in touch with the scattered

family. . . . A clergyman appeared and wandered about aimlessly, and someone played the piano.'

The number of homeless had been swollen by the government's initial decision to evacuate all premises within 600 yards of an unexploded bomb (UXB) and to close all roads within the danger area. This was a policy dictated by caution, as many of the UXBs were not duds but fitted with delayed-action fuses. The result was that many thousands of people were abruptly excluded from their homes and prevented from returning to them after work or a night in the shelters. They were forced to join the ranks of the homeless in the Rest Centres, frequently living in limbo for days while the hard-pressed bomb disposal units fought to clear the backlog of UXBs, which by November had risen to 3000.

At first it was left to heroic individuals to sustain morale and provide the homeless with food and shelter. Voluntary workers begged, borrowed and stole blankets, clothes, food and coal. In West Ham there was no provision for communal feeding. The owner of a local pieshop came to the rescue. His own premises had been bombed out, but with great ingenuity he repaired his oven with some old drainpipes caulked together with dough. The next day he provided 2700 hungry East Enders with a dinner of soup, meat pie and potatoes and bread at 4d a head.

A Rest Centre in Islington was invaded by a formidable red-faced woman who sold beetroots in the market. She immediately took control, providing milk for the babies, bedding them down with their mothers and then producing a powder which within minutes resulted in a miraculous quiet. Then she turned her attention to the elderly and infirm, ensuring that they were allotted beds for the night. By the time the bombs began to fall, her 103 gratefully bemused charges were either asleep or dozing. In the morning she organized washing, bathed the babies, swept the floor and cooked breakfast. In a single night this remarkable woman had transformed a scene of dismal chaos into a welcoming haven for those recovering from the shock of being bombed out.

It was not long before the Ministry of Health and the London County Council stepped in to expand and improve the Rest Centres. By November the majority had become clean and well-organized places, capable of fulfilling their intended function, providing washing facilities, dispensing food and clothing and advice.

The first raids came closest to undermining civilian morale. On 17 September Harold Nicolson, then Parliamentary Secretary to the Ministry of Information, wrote in his diary: 'There is much bitterness. It is said that even the King and Queen were booed when they visited the devastated areas.' At the beginning of the Blitz there was a sharp contrast between the largely untouched West End, where Lord Halifax had his specially reserved bunk in the deep shelter at the Dorchester Hotel, and the acres of shattered tenements in the East End.

On 15 September about a hundred East Enders, led by Communists, gathered outside the Savoy Hotel, whose underground banqueting hall had been converted into a restaurant-dormitory for its guests. When the first siren sounded the group rushed the hotel and demanded that they should be accommodated in the hotel's new shelter. With some reluctance they were admitted, but the demonstration was frustrated when the all-clear sounded a few minutes later. The Savoy was full of journalists at the time and the incident received considerable coverage abroad, not least in Germany, where it was triumphantly cited as an indication of the imminent collapse of the British social order.

But there was no revolution. Soon the West End was receiving its own

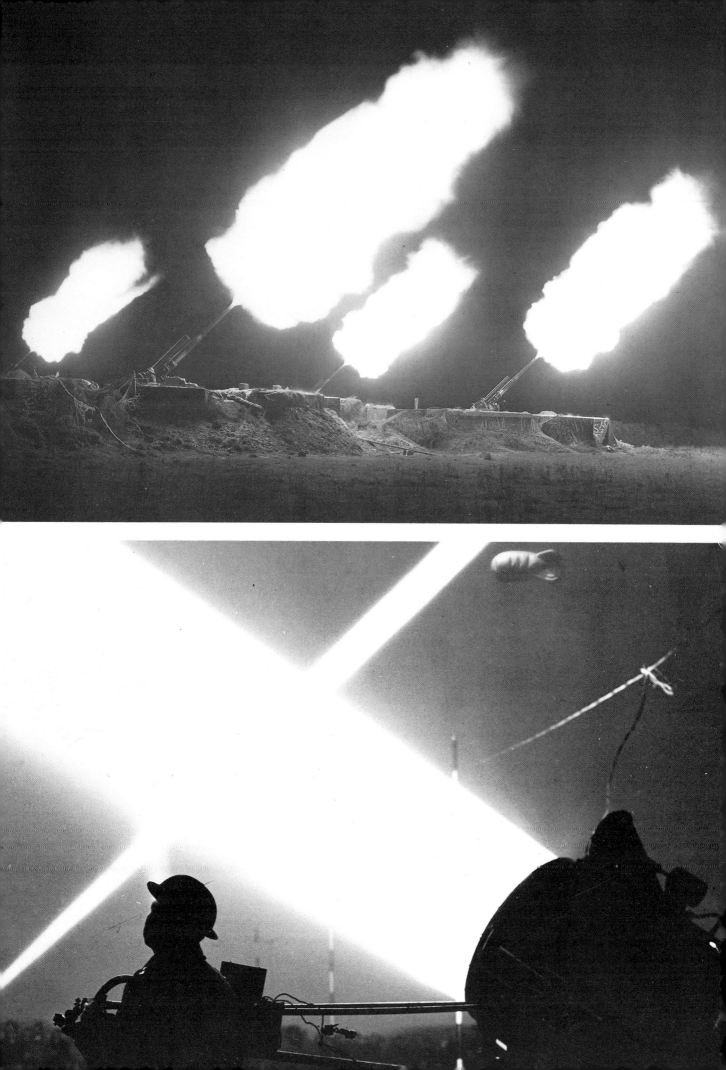

Opposite, top and bottom: In April 1941 Winston Churchill declared, 'I see the damage done by the enemy attacks; but I also see, side by side with the devastation and the ruins, quiet, confident, bright and smiling eyes, beaming with consciousness of being associated with a cause far higher and wider than any human or personal issue. I can see the spirit of an unquenchable people'.

share of bombs. On 13 September the Luftwaffe struck an unintentional blow for democracy by bombing Buckingham Palace, demonstrating that all Londoners, high or low, faced the same dangers. This single incident, during a night when 181 bombers dropped 224 tons of high explosive and 279 incendiary canisters on London, awoke a strong feeling of solidarity among all classes of people in the capital and prompted the Queen to make the famous remark, 'I'm glad that we've been bombed. It makes me feel that I can look the East End in the face.'

After the first battering, morale held. It was boosted by the energetic commander of AA Command, General Sir Frederick Pile, who reinforced his batteries with guns from the provinces and instructed every gun to fire every possible round at the German raiders. The 'barrage', as it became known, had a twofold effect. First, and most important, the colossal cacophony it raised every night convinced Londoners that the air defences were finally hitting back at the enemy. The barrage accounted for few German aircraft; in fact, more civilians were killed by shell fragments than were enemy aircrew. But its ferocity, however inaccurate, forced the bombers to fly higher, dispersing their effort and easing the task of the overburdened Civil Defence services. Not everyone welcomed the barrage. One suburban local authority wrote to General Pile complaining that the vibrations the guns were creating were cracking the lavatory bowls in its council houses.

Two weeks into the Blitz, Londoners were acclimatizing to a life under bombardment. People were still frightened in a heavy raid, but they were learning how to control themselves. Watching the occupants of a shelter in Exmouth Street, Stepney, an area which was hit very badly on 18 September, an air warden noted: 'They got over it. A dreadful shock, and they got over it quickly. They kept bringing people in from Exmouth Street, though, and it got *very* hot.' A young girl in the same shelter movingly confided to her neighbours, 'Everyone was frightened, but they controlled themselves. Hetty cried, but she cried quietly, and no one saw her. Gertie fainted, but she fainted at the back and didn't make a fuss. . . . I'm glad my parents aren't here. My mother would have been hysterical.'

As the weeks passed people discovered with amazement that, in spite of the bombs, life was bearable. For some it provided a sudden surge of excitement in a humdrum life. A middle-aged worker in a small London factory making ornamental buttons was asked, after he had been bombed out twice, if he and his wife would like to be evacuated as non-essential personnel. 'What and miss all this?' was his reply. '[Not] for all the gold in China! There's never been nothing like it! Never! And never will be again!'

The bombing became the background to everyday life and a shared experience. Every street now knew the reality of modern warfare, and everyone had their own bomb story, often reflecting the feeling of excitement which gripped those who had emerged unscathed from a brush with death. A Mass-Observer recorded a conversation between five male residents of Mill Hill following a severe raid at the end of September:

> 'It was an awful night, I expect you heard about it; it was in the news. I was up half the night with incendiaries – the ARP couldn't cope and we all turned out to help. . . . We got a packet our way. . . . I thought I'd feel like death this morning – but I don't. I feel marvellous – on top of the world.'
>
> 'We were coming home [from an ARP training class] last night, and about a quarter of a mile ahead a green flame sprang up, and we knew they were incendiaries! We were as pleased as punch!'

Above: Bombed-out office workers don tin helmets and carry on with the typing.

'I found a bomb – an incendiary – outside my house which hadn't gone off, so I rushed indoors and found a shovel to cover the bomb with earth. It was a brand-new shovel; and I was just putting down the earth . . . and it suddenly blew off! It burnt the hair off my hands and broke my shovel in two! Did I swear at blasted Jerry then! My new shovel! I'd been enjoying it until that happened!'

'I helped to put out three. When I got in, my old woman pushed a heap of chips in front of me and said, "Eat those!" I never enjoyed anything so much in all my life.'

'I wouldn't mind having an evening like it say once a week. Ordinarily, there's no excitement, nothing to do or anything.'

Londoners quickly learned to combine the continuing routines of normal life – turning up for work, feeding the family, stepping out with the boyfriend, enjoying a drink in the local pub – with the strange sensations of the Blitz. There was the rising wail of the warning sirens, followed by the menacing throb of the approaching bombers – the writer Graham Greene imagined them growling, 'Where are you? Where are you?'; the sound of high-explosive bombs falling, likened to a tearing sheet; the rattle of incendiaries on roofs and streets; the splatter of shrapnel on the pavements. Overhead, searchlights swept a sky which, in a big raid, was suffused with the livid colours of a tropical sunset. Descending parachute flares suddenly bathed the streets in a sinister green light. Incendiaries hissed and burned with a blueish-white or green glare. In his memoirs the splendidly named Sir Aylmer Firebrace, Chief of the Fire Staff with London Region during the Blitz, recalled the experience of being in the centre of a concentration of incendiaries: 'One moment the street would be dark, the next it would be illuminated by a hundred sizzling blueish-white flames. They made a curious plop-plopping sound as they fell on roads and pavements, but this was not

Opposite: The Anderson shelter was strong enough to survive almost everything short of a direct hit. Remembering nights spent in the Anderson shelter, the historian Norman Longmate wrote, 'To be inside an Anderson shelter felt rather like being entombed in a small, dark bicycle shed, smelling of earth and damp'.

often heard above the shrill whirring noise made by the pumps. They never gave me the impression that they had been dropped from the skies – they seemed rather to have sprouted.'

At first incendiaries could be easily smothered with sand or a sandbag; they could even be picked up with a pair of heavy tongs or heavy gloves, deposited in an empty bucket and carried away to a safe place. Those that fell on a roadway or a stone roof could be left to burn themselves out. However, from December 1940 one in ten incendiaries dropped by the Luftwaffe contained a small explosive charge, making each one a potentially lethal grenade which could maim or kill those who tried to dispose of it. Dealing with incendiaries ceased to be something of an adventure and became, quite literally, a matter of life and death. Left to their own devices, the incendiaries would quickly start a blaze.

Underfoot, the bombed-out streets were frosted with millions of fragments of broken glass, a phenomenon which gradually disappeared as windows were blown out and shop fronts boarded up, the plate glass front being replaced by a peephole. After a raid the nostrils were assailed by the acrid smell of a bombed-out street, an unforgettable mixture of dust, smoke, charred timber and escaping gas described by John Strachey as 'the smell of violent death itself'.

The casually unpredictable side effects of bomb blast could turn the urban scene into a dreamscape. All those who lived through the Blitz recall the disturbing sight of a house torn open to reveal, in the bright autumn sunshine, the lives and possessions of its occupants in pathetic, dust-shrouded disorder. William Sansom tells the story of a Westminster man who, arriving home very late, failed to notice that his house had been neatly sliced in two. He climbed the stairs and, fortunately for him, went to bed in the half of his bedroom that was still standing. He was brought down by a ladder.

Bomb blast could mangle the bodies of its victims or, capriciously, leave a human being unhurt but stripped naked. The trees in London's squares were often decorated with a random variety of items borne aloft by the blast. Walking through Hyde Park, Inez Holden saw, 'The highest branch of a tree draped with bits of marabout, with some sort of silk, with two or three odd stockings and, wrapped round the top of a tree, like a cloak quick-thrown over the shoulder of some high-born hidalgo, some purple damask. Below it, balanced on a twig as if twirled round a finger, was a brand new bowler hat.' On one memorable occasion a direct hit on Madame Tussaud's scattered wax 'corpses' across the street outside.

A bizarre incident occurred at the Granada Cinema, Welling, on the southeastern approach to London. The building was caught in a heavy fall of incendiaries, several of which crashed through the roof during the Sunday evening show. While the staff battled with the incendiaries inside the cinema, chief operator Ted White stood by on the roof. Eventually he telephoned down, 'Stand by to abandon the cinema. Everything's alight but us,' and, looking down on the fires which ringed the theatre, he saw what he took to be a new secret weapon – little balls of fire darting about in every back garden in sight; they were hens burning.

The new routines for living were woven around the nightly routine of being bombed. Among the most enduring images of the Blitz are those of the shelters: the platform of a Tube station packed from end to end with fitfully slumbering humanity; or a family huddled together in the damp intimacy of their Anderson shelter. However, a survey undertaken in November 1940 revealed the remarkable fact that only 40 per cent of

Londoners regularly went to a shelter at night during a raid. Displaying a mixture of optimism and fatalism, the majority of the population stayed in their beds or under the stairs.

Twenty-seven per cent of those who chose to take shelter slept in their Anderson, the most widely used domestic shelter throughout the Blitz. The Anderson was built to survive almost everything but a direct hit. But it tended to flood, and pumping out the Anderson became a frequent and wearisome chore for London's firemen. Wartime economies meant that many of the later batches were too small to sleep in. Nor did they shut out the ferocious din of a raid. Vera Lynn recalls, 'a particularly bad raid spent crammed in a neighbour's shelter in Barking. We felt safe and insulated from all that was going on outside, except the noise! But the cramped conditions and discomfort often led to a dash back into the house to fetch a drink or an extra blanket. At the height of a raid it was best to stay put. On this occasion the big bus depot just around the corner took a direct hit and was completely destroyed. When the all-clear sounded we emerged from the shelter to find the garden littered with ugly hunks of concrete which had been hurled over the rooftops when the bus depot went up. Had I been making a dash for it at that moment, I would have been crushed under the weight of falling masonry.'

Nine per cent of Londoners took refuge in public shelters. The government's pre-war policy had been to disperse the population in an air raid rather than build a network of large public shelters which might become mass tombs. It had also shrunk from providing a system of deep underground shelters, fearing that thousands of demoralized civilians would take to living permanently underground. Originally the principal public shelters were squat surface brick and concrete shelters of spectacular inadequacy. These communal shelters were designed to house approximately fifty local residents and passers-by. They were dank, unsanitary places, whose poor construction turned them into death traps when a bomb burst nearby. Frequently the roof, a concrete slab, was lifted by the blast to come crashing down on the insecurely mortared walls which fell in on the occupants. The problem was remedied by improved mortaring, the building of an outer blast wall and the edging of the concrete roof so that it overlapped the shelter's sides and could shift a few inches without falling off its supports.

The brick shelters were never popular, prompting some forlorn government efforts to widen their appeal, including this leaflet, issued by the Ministry of Home Security, 'Your Brick Street Shelter This Winter':

A brick street shelter decorated with the local community's own ironic comments.

You and your neighbours can easily make your brick street shelter into a place where you can spend many hours at night, not only in comfort but under conditions where your family's health and your own will not suffer. . . . There is a great deal you can do at little or no cost to make the shelter healthy and homelike. You can begin by getting some old rolls of wallpaper – shopkeepers often have some they are willing to sell for a few pence. Paper the walls of your shelter and whitewash the ceiling. A home-made heater can be made with two large flower pots and a candle. . . . A balaclava helmet, such as every soldier knows, will keep draughts off your head. . . . By far the best bedding for any shelter is a properly made sleeping bag. . . . Take any army or similar thick blanket about 7 feet long and 6 feet 6 inches wide, . . . line with muslin or cotton material making pockets, which should be well stuffed with old newspaper.

Clearly the Men from the Ministry believed that not only an Englishman's home, but also his brick street communal shelter, was his castle.

Many people preferred the trenches dug in the parks, some of them dating from the Munich crisis. They were lined and roofed with concrete or steel and were equipped with closed entrances, but initially had no duckboards, seats or sanitary facilities. Like the Andersons, they were liable to flood, but they proved more popular than the street shelters with the public, who felt safer underground, with three feet of earth over their heads.

Local authorities also improvised shelters in the basements of strong buildings. In Paddington, for example, forty public shelters were created in existing buildings, in addition to the borough's eleven surface shelters and four trenches. On any one night 76,000 of Paddington's citizens could take shelter – 21,000 of them in their Andersons and the remainder in other types of domestic or communal shelter.

Then there were the 'self-chosen' shelters, taken over by people on their own initiative. Every night thousands of Londoners took special trains to Chislehurst Caves, in Kent, which were soon crammed with creature comforts – armchairs, double beds, even a barber's shop. In London, unofficial shelters – which were chosen because of their size and seeming strength – offered a safety which was frequently illusory.

The spaces beneath railway arches were a favourite refuge, perhaps the most notorious of which was the Tilbury Shelter, off the Commercial Road in Stepney, which was part of the Liverpool Street goods yard and had been used as a shelter in the First World War. Its roof, supported by rows of giant arches, gave an impression of vast solidity and a section had been converted by the local council into a shelter for 3000 people. Thousands more poured into an unofficial and unreinforced section, in the loading yard of a huge warehouse. It was estimated that every night over 10,000 people sheltered here among massive government stocks of margarine, a teeming twilight world of strangers.

Ritchie Calder visited the Tilbury Shelter in its early days:

People queued up from midday, waiting for the gates to open at 4.30 in the afternoon. Service men on leave kept places for their families out at work. Unevacuated schoolchildren were 'proxies' for their relatives. Old folk in bathchairs, cripples, children in perambulators, and men and women of every age and condition lined up, oblivious of daylight sirens and even dogfights overhead, because if they took shelter they lost their places in the queue and their 'option' on their favourite sleeping spot for the night. When the gates were opened the police linked hands to stem the rush down the slope, but it was like holding back a stampede of buffalos. Usually a way was made for the aged, and for mothers with perambulators and young children (although the police got wise to the fact that they were getting priority for perambulators which contained not babies, but the family valuables). Sometimes women and children got crushed in the rush.

At night it presented a scene unequalled by anything west of Suez. One had to pick one's way along the roads between the recumbent bodies. Until the Ministry of Food intervened and had the cartons of margarine and the other foodstuffs removed, people slept in the bays, beside or on the food. To begin with there was practically no sanitary provision, and the filth seeped into the blankets or was spread by trampling feet. Cartons filled with margarine were sometimes stacked up to form latrines.

Every race and colour in the world were represented there – Whites, Negroes, Chinese, Hindus, Polynesians, Levantines, East Europeans, Jews, Gentiles, Moslems, and probably sun-worshippers were all piled up there in miscellaneous confusion. Seamen came in for a few hours between tides. Prostitutes paraded. Hawkers sold clammy fried fish, which cloyed the fug with greasy sickliness. The police broke up free fights. And children slept.

Opposite, top: It was not long before the Londoners sheltering in the Tube system organised their own routines and entertainments. With the current cut off in the electric rail, a crowd gathers for a singalong. *Bottom, left:* Bedding down for the night on the rails. *Bottom, right:* A troubled sleep, and a stiff back in the morning, for those who chose the escalator.

Gradually the shelterers evolved a rough-and-ready set of rules, enforced by self-appointed shelter marshals, which brought order to the Tilbury Shelter. Passageways were kept clear and gangways were left through every arch; music and singing in the main part of the shelter were stopped after 10 p.m.; 'places' were respected, but a limit was imposed on the space occupied by a single person; it was an unpardonable sin to tread on anyone's blanket. Simultaneously the authorities supplied sanitary facilities and a small army of cleaners to clear up in the morning. As time went by people developed a fierce loyalty to the bay in which they regularly slept and to their fellow-occupants. Interlopers who dropped their blankets on a seemingly empty space were quickly sent packing.

A similar process took place in another huge unofficial shelter in Stepney, popularly known as 'Mickey's Shelter', after the remarkable Mickey Davis, a tiny hunchbacked East End optician whose inspirational leadership ensured the election of a shelter committee and the donation of a canteen by Marks and Spencer. When the American politician Wendell Wilkie visited London in the autumn of 1940 he was taken on a tour of Mickey's Shelter as an example of British grassroots democracy at work.

The remaining 4 per cent of those who took shelter every night went underground, into the London Tube system. At the beginning of the war the government had rejected the use of the Tubes as shelters, fearful of creating a 'deep shelter' mentality and wishing to keep every line of transport clear for troop movements. But there was nothing illegal about buying a platform ticket for 1½d and then not travelling. Without any great disorder the public overruled the authorities, bought their platform tickets and camped on the platforms.

The Tubes were dry and insulated from the noise of the bombing. The authorities relented, initially closing a branch line to the Aldwych and opening it to the shelterers. Then three disused stations were opened, followed by an uncompleted extension at Liverpool Street which could accommodate 10,000 people. Ultimately eighty stations in Greater London became *de facto* shelters; at their peak in late September they were housing 177,000 people every night.

As with the Tilbury Shelter, a routine was swiftly established. Queues formed outside the Tube shelters early in the morning, with children or servicemen on leave waiting patiently in line to establish priority for their families. Spivs turned a tidy profit by selling places in the queue and on the platform, the latter costing 2s 6d, or more if the raid hotted up. Down below, transport officials attempted to keep the platforms clear by painting two white lines, one 8 feet and the other 4 feet from the platform's edge. Before 7.30 p.m. the shelterers were not supposed to cross the 8-foot line. After this the barrier moved forward to the 4-foot line until 10.30 p.m., when the trains stopped running, the lights were dimmed and the current was cut off in the electric rail. The shelterers could now settle down to sleep on the platforms, the passageways, the escalators and even between the rails. Legend has it that their snoring rose and fell like a loud wind. The all-clear usually sounded before 6 a.m., and by 7 o'clock the Tube was back to normal, with the station staffs clearing away the mounds of rubbish left behind by the shelterers.

Sheltering in the Tube was a far from comfortable experience. There was a plague of mosquitoes, encouraged out of hibernation in the warm fug generated by the packed bodies of the shelterers. The conditions also provided lice with a happy hunting ground. Alternate hot and cold blasts of wind raced through the tunnels. Below the level of the sewage mains

In the early days of the Blitz there was little chance of Brockbank's cartoon prediction becoming reality. Conditions for those spending a night as guests of the London Underground were extremely uncomfortable. Later, the introduction of improved sanitary facilities and the provision of medical care and bunks made up for many of the initial deficiencies.

"*What did I tell you? Give them an inch and they take a mile.*"

there were no toilet or washing facilities; people walked into the tunnels to relieve themselves and the stench was sometimes overwhelming.

Nor were all Tube stations as safe as they seemed. Deep underground the shelterers were protected against the bombs, but nearer the surface they became increasingly vulnerable. There were a number of harrowing incidents, the worst of which occurred at Balham Station, whose roof was only 30 feet beneath the Balham High Road. About six hundred were sheltering there on the night of 14 October when a direct hit burst the water main running directly overhead and flooded the station. Those who were not killed by the bomb blast were drowned.

Sillince pokes whimsical fun at the Morrison shelter. Introduced in 1941, it was named after Herbert Morrison, Minister of Home Security. A family shelter, free for most people, it could be erected indoors. It had a steel plate on top, which could be used as a table in the daytime, and sides of wire mesh 2ft 9in high. Over half a million had been distributed by November 1941.

"*By the way, did you remember to feed the canary?*"

By the end of September the government was considering a report on conditions in the shelters drawn up by a committee under the chairmanship of Lord Horder. The committee was particularly concerned to prevent the outbreak of a serious epidemic in the unsanitary conditions which prevailed in many shelters, and among its detailed recommendations were measures against overcrowding and the provision of first-aid posts and medical supervision in the big shelters. Acting on the report, the government had installed 600,000 bunks in the shelters by April 1941. The introduction of these three-tier wooden (later metal) frames was resented in many shelters, as they cut down the space available and forced many people to leave a favourite haven and seek a new refuge.

Improved sanitary facilities and the provision of medical care prevented the outbreak of the epidemics which had so worried the Horder Committee. The government and local authorities also encouraged the introduction of social amenities. In Bermondsey a company of amateur actors toured the shelters with a production of Chekhov's *The Bear*; at Swiss Cottage the shelterers produced their own magazine, *The Swiss Cottager*; in some boroughs the Women's Voluntary Service (WVS) organized lectures and spelling bees. In South London the men of 167 Company, Pioneer Corps, got up a concert party which performed in the shelters six nights a week for thirteen weeks. Library services were provided – in West Ham 4000 paperbacks went out on loan – and film shows were a regular feature of the larger shelters. By January 1940 the LCC was holding more than 200 classes in the shelters, ranging from current affairs to dressmaking. The Council for the Encouragement of Music and the Arts (CEMA) supplied gramophones, classical records and earnest lecturers whose job it was 'to explain the meaning of the music and the circumstances in which it was written'. Even more remarkable were the circumstances in which it was now heard.

In October 1940 the government reversed its policy on deep shelters. Work was begun on eight deep-level shelters, connected to Tube stations, each of which was to be capable of housing 8000 people. None of these had been completed by the time the Blitz ended in May 1941. They were subsequently used in the V-weapon campaign which began in the summer of 1944, and also provided billets for troops and General Eisenhower with his D-Day invasion offices.

Improvements to existing shelters ensured that by the end of February 1941 there was public shelter space for 1.4 million people in the London region. A month later the government introduced the Morrison shelter (named after Herbert Morrison, the Minister of Home Security), a box-like structure topped with a steel plate for indoor use. Few had been delivered by the end of the Blitz, but the Morrison shelter gave sterling service later in the war and was capable of withstanding the collapse of a two-storey house.

Throughout September 1940 London had taken a terrible hammering, but its sheer size prevented the Luftwaffe from delivering a knockout blow to civilian morale – later in the war RAF Bomber Command experienced the same problem over Berlin. Nor was London the centre of British industrial production. Its docks area had been heavily bombed, but in spite of its size and importance it was still only one among many. The influx of foodstuffs and war material had not slackened appreciably since the beginning of the German onslaught. In October the Luftwaffe turned its attention to the Midlands and the North, the home of British heavy industry. Among the major targets were Liverpool, Birmingham and the city of Coventry, Luftwaffe Target No. 53.

Figures in a bomb-blasted landscape clamber over a Morrison shelter which, although buckled, remains intact.

83

Left: A wartime cladding of sandbags for the Flamingo House at Bristol Zoo. The animals stood up well to the Blitz, as they did at London Zoo. Nevertheless, as a precaution all the poisonous snakes and reptiles were destroyed, lest they escape during a raid. *Right:* The shell of Coventry Cathedral, gutted during the raid of 14/15 November 1940. In spite of the devastation caused by the Luftwaffe, Coventry's factories were back in full production within a matter of days.

Left: 'Trekkers' leaving Southampton in December 1940. The government was worried that the nightly exodus from provincial cities under attack was evidence of a failure of morale. It was wrong; the overwhelming majority of 'trekkers' returned to work the next morning, often after spending a night in the open.

Left: The city centre of Plymouth in the immediate postwar years, still showing the destruction caused by the German raids.

Late in the afternoon of 14 November an aircraft of No. 80 Wing, the RAF's Radio Countermeasures Unit, intercepted a German radio navigation 'X beam' laid across the Midlands, an area which had thus far escaped heavy night raids. This provided confirmation of an Air Intelligence forecast that the Germans were planning a big night offensive, *Mondscheinserenade* (Moonlight Serenade), to take advantage of the full moon.

Less than two hours later the opening blow fell when the first of 449 bombers appeared over Coventry, marking the way for the main force with incendiaries. In the ensuing eleven-hour attack, conducted in the excellent visibility of a clear, frosty night, 503 tons of high explosives and 30,000 incendiaries were dropped on Coventry. There were 554 civilian casualties and 1200 injured; 70,000 buildings were either damaged or destroyed; three-quarters of the city centre was razed; the medieval cathedral was gutted. In the immediate aftermath of the raid the feeling was that 'Coventry is finished.'

Two days later Tom Harrisson described the scene in Coventry on the BBC's Home Service: 'The strangest sight of all was the cathedral. At each end the bare frames of the great windows still have a kind of beauty without their glass; but in between them there is an incredible chaos of bricks, pillars, girders and memorial tablets. And all through the town there's damage – rows and rows of houses, smashed-in windows and leaking roofs. (Nearly one-third of all homes have been made uninhabitable.)

'As soon as darkness fell, the streets were silent. The people of Coventry had gone to shelter. For more than an hour I drove in my car picking a way through craters and glass, and during the whole time I saw no other private car. I think this is one of the weirdest experiences of my whole life, driving in a lonely, silent desolation and drizzling rain in that great industrial town. Then I met a gang of young men looking for a drink. I went with them because I wanted one too. We must have visited half the pubs in Coventry before we found one.'

Twenty-one of Coventry's factories – twelve of them connected with the aircraft industry – had been severely damaged. In addition, the city's public utilities – its telephones, gas, water, electricity and transport systems – had been thrown into chaos. In turn, this brought to a standstill a number of factories which had escaped serious bomb damage. It had been the obliteration of the heart of the city, rather than the precision bombing of the factories, which had temporarily paralysed Coventry's war effort and thrown the local government and population into a state of shock. If the Luftwaffe had returned on three successive nights (a task which would have been made easier by the fires still burning from previous attacks), a vital sector of Britain's war economy might have been dealt a crippling blow. But the Luftwaffe did not return, shifting its attention first to London and then to Southampton, which received the first in series of heavy raids on 17 November. Coventry was not hit hard again until 8 April 1941.

Coventry was not finished. In London the scale of the city masked the effects of the bombing; but in a medium-sized city like Coventry, with a population of about 220,000, the comprehensiveness of the destruction was there for all to see. In London many of the capital's oldest focal buildings were never destroyed, most famously St Paul's Cathedral, Westminster Abbey and Buckingham Palace. In Coventry everything went up in flames in a single night. Paradoxically, the disaster which befell Coventry produced a swelling local pride in the scale of the destruction which echoed at a community level the strong emotions many individuals felt when they were bombed. Out of the ruins grew a determination not to knuckle under. At the end of November a commercial traveller, who regularly visited Coventry, noted in his diary that, after a period of 'feeling helpless at first . . . having got over the initial shock, I think they are now prepared to *stand anything*.'

Most of Coventry's factories were back in production within days. The weeks following the raid demonstrated the remarkable resilience under aerial bombardment of both civilians and industrial plant. Shattered dwellings did not remove the work force who, in the final analysis, simply had to keep on earning a living to support their families; and under shattered factory roofs vital machine tools often survived intact. The bombers had got through. They had inflicted terrible damage. But they had won only a qualified victory. Never again was the Luftwaffe to throw so many aircraft against a provincial industrial town. Clydeside came nearest, with an attack by 386 aircraft on 5 May 1941 when the Blitz had nearly run its course.

The raids on Britain's provincial cities produced a phenomenon known as 'trekking'. Every night the trekkers left their home towns in thousands, seeking the safety of the surrounding countryside, sleeping where they could and returning in the morning. This uncontrolled form of evacuation was first noted at Southampton, which suffered five heavy raids between 17 November 1940 and 19 January 1941. At dusk the trekkers moved off into the zones beyond the wail of the siren, placing an extra strain on already disrupted transport systems. Taxis, private cars and even buses became private dormitories parked in country lanes. Bicycles suddenly became prized items. On 2 December, after being bombed for two successive nights, Southampton seemed like a ghost town, and a visitor leaving the train at the docks that evening was struck by 'the seeming deadness of the town . . . no cars and hardly any people'.

These nightly mass migrations were repeated across Britain. In Plymouth, badly hit in March and April 1941, up to 50,000 trekked into the sparsely populated hinterland to sleep in barns, farmhouses, churches, quarry tunnels, ditches and on the windswept fringes of Dartmoor. On 1 May the *Plymouth Herald* commented: 'Tonight some of the city's streets are nothing more than a desert of dusty rubble. They are streets that the citizens leave for the countryside when the night falls.' When the shipbuilding town of Clydebank came under heavy attack in mid-March 1941 the town's nocturnal population dropped overnight from 50,000 to 2000. On Merseyside in the spring of 1941 the five successive nights of 'May Week', ending on 7 May, produced a mass exodus.

The government did not approve of trekking and attempted to ignore it, declining to provide any help for trekking families who were not homeless. The long lines of civilians trudging out of Britain's cities every night were depressingly reminiscent of the columns of refugees who clogged the roads before the fall of France and hinted at a collapse in morale. The phenomenon was particularly evident at Plymouth, where a narrow isthmus connected the main part of the port town to the mainland. However, the impression was misleading; for many people trekking was the only solution available at times when local services were overwhelmed by the ferocity of a heavy attack. When the dawn came up they creaked stiffly to their feet and returned to their jobs. It was not until May 1941 that the government sanctioned improvements to rural Rest Centres. By then the need for them had largely passed with the ending of the heavy raids.

The dome of St Paul's Cathedral rises majestic and unscathed above the fires raised at the height of the incendiary attack on London on 29 December, 1940.

During the Blitz on London there was only one occasion on which the Luftwaffe threatened to create conditions similar to those which, after Allied raids, were to lead to the terrible firestorms in Hamburg (1943) and Dresden (1945). On Sunday, 29 December 1940, an incendiary raid on the City of London was compounded by a neap-tide, which made it all but impossible for the hoses of the fire brigade to reach down to the river. Shops and offices were locked up and the firewatchers, who were still volunteers, off duty. The two-hour attack, by the relatively small number of 150 aircraft, started some 1500 fires, of which 90 per cent raged virtually unchecked in the City, fanned by a strong westerly wind. One conflagration, which consumed everything between Moorgate, Aldersgate Street, Cannon Street and Old Street, produced the biggest area of war devastation in Great Britain.

On the edge of this sea of fire stood St Paul's Cathedral, its dome rising majestically above the dense clouds of black smoke. St Paul's was hit by at least twenty-eight incendiaries, one of which stuck halfway through the outer shell of the dome. Had it fallen through onto the beams and dry timbers of the inner dome, St Paul's might well have burned down. Miraculously the incendiary suddenly slid off and fell on to the Stone Gallery, where it was quickly extinguished.

That night a Bethnal Green woman had donned her tin hat and ventured into the inferno in the City. 'I went up on the roof with some of the firemen to look at the City. And I've always remembered how I was choked, I think I was crying a little. I could see St Paul's standing there, and the fire all around, and I just said, "Please God, don't let it go!" I couldn't help it, I felt that if St Paul's had gone, something would have gone from us. But it stood in defiance, it did. And when the boys were coming back, the firemen said, "It's bad, but, oh, the old church stood it." Lovely, that was.'

The final phase of the Blitz began in mid-April 1941, with a raid on London by 685 aircraft, and ended with a savage raid on the capital by 507 bombers on the night of 10–11 May in which 700 tons of high explosives and incendiaries were dropped, starting 2200 fires from Hammersmith to Romford and killing 1436. The next morning a third of the streets of London were impassable and 155,000 families were left without gas, water or electricity. The last pumps were not withdrawn from the fires until 21 May.

Sixteen enemy aircraft had been destroyed by the air defences on the night of 10–11 May, the highest total in a single night during the campaign. However, these losses were not sufficient to bring a halt to the night offensive against Britain. Rather, it was the transfer to the East of units earmarked for the invasion of the Soviet Union, which Hitler launched on 22 June. By the end of June two-thirds of the Luftwaffe had been withdrawn from the campaign against Britain and the grinding routine of raids on her cities was replaced by 'tip and run' fighter–bomber attacks on coastal towns. After a comparative lull the Germans opened a new offensive in the spring of 1942, principally as a reprisal against RAF Bomber Command's destruction of the ancient Baltic city of Lubeck on 28–29 March. The campaign was aimed at Britain's historic towns, notably Exeter, Bath, Norwich, York and Canterbury. The attacks quickly earned the nickname 'Baedeker raids', on the assumption that the targets had been chosen from the well-known tourist guides.

The Baedeker raids were not large by the standards of the Blitz: the biggest was mounted by some ninety bombers against Exeter on 3 May. But they reproduced the effects of the Blitz on small, weakly defended cities, previously untouched by the air war, whose post-raid services had not been worked up to the state of readiness which now prevailed in Britain's major cities. At Canterbury, for example, which was raided on 31 May and then on 2 and 6 June, there were fewer than a hundred casualties, but volunteer workers toiled for months to help the homeless, and in the following September 800 men were still at work repairing damaged houses. However, harrowing as it was for the inhabitants of Canterbury, the damage done to their beautiful city by the Luftwaffe was as nothing compared with the 600 acres of devastation which Bomber Command left behind after the 'Thousand Bomber' raid on Cologne on 30–31 May, only hours before Canterbury was hit for the first time. Hitler had sown the whirlwind; now the German people were reaping the whirlwind.

By the late spring of 1941 the Blitz had reached a point almost of stalemate. Britain's air defences, initially powerless, had significantly improved, principally because of the introduction of radar-equipped ground-directed night fighters and the vigorous upgrading of AA Command by General Pile. In December 1940 one bomber in every 326 had been brought down; in January 1941 the figure had fallen to one in every 100; in February the average had been reduced to one in every 95; and at the beginning of March one in every 63. But the Luftwaffe could have sustained these losses indefinitely and at the same time have continued to inflict severe damage on Britain's cities and industries. Not until February 1941 did British aircraft production creep back up to the level which

London Can Take It. A soldier makes his point with a stained glass panel retrieved from a bomb-damaged pub after the raid of 29 December, 1940.

Above: A tide of fierce emotion runs through mourners at the mass funeral of children killed when their school took a direct hit.

Opposite: The sinister shape of an unexploded parachute mine.

it had reached in August 1940, on the eve of the Blitz. But the British war effort soaked up the punishment, and the overall effect on production remained negligible. The apocalyptic predictions of the 1930s had been proved false. London remained the nation's administrative and economic capital; Portsmouth and Plymouth continued to service the Royal Navy; although they took a terrible hammering, the Liverpool docks stayed open, the vital last link in Britain's Atlantic supply chain; and Coventry absorbed the trauma of 14–15 November 1940 to *increase* its war production.

The price of survival was high. Some 40,000 civilians had been killed in the Blitz proper. In 1940 London bore the brunt of casualties, with 13,596 deaths from enemy action compared with a total of 10,171 for all other British towns and cities. Throughout 1941 the death toll ran higher outside London – 13,431 killed in the provinces compared with 6487 in the capital.

None of Britain's provincial cities had been subjected to a bombardment lasting longer than eight consecutive nights. The Luftwaffe's constant switching of targets provided a crucial breathing space to battered populations whose local post-raid services had proved unequal to dealing with the havoc caused by a heavy raid. Londoners, however, had lived through fifty-seven consecutive nights of bombing and had then endured a further seventy-six consecutive nights. Between September 1940 and May 1941 London received approximately 19,000 tons of high explosives and incendiaries, 13,000 of which fell between September and

mid-November 1940. As the campaign wore on the Luftwaffe used bigger and more destructive bombs, including at least 4000 500- or 1000-kg sea mines (often incorrectly termed land mines) attached to parachutes. These 8-foot cylinders floated lazily down with a deceptive lack of urgency before exploding on impact with a huge radius of blast which very few who were near it survived.

One who survived the mine which destroyed the Langham Hotel recalled the incident in a wartime recording made by the BBC. He was standing outside Broadcasting House when he:

'noticed a large, dark, shiny object approach the lamp post [in the middle of the road] and then recede. I concluded that it was a taxi parking. It made no noise. The night was clear, with a few small clouds. There was moonlight from a westerly direction, but Portland Place was mainly shadow. All three of us were wearing our steel helmets; my chinstrap was round the back of my head, as I had been advised to wear it so shortly after I had been issued with the helmet. . . . A few seconds later I saw what seemed to be a very large tarpaulin of a drab or khaki colour fall on the same spot; the highest part of it was about ten or twelve feet above the road when I first saw it, and it seemed to be about twenty-five feet across. It fell about the speed of a pocket handkerchief when dropped and made no noise. Repair work was being carried out on Broadcasting House and I, not unnaturally, concluded that it was a tarpaulin which had become detached from the building and fallen into the roadway. . . . I went towards the tarpaulin and had reached a spot to the left of Clarke [a policeman] and about six feet from the curb, and twenty-five to thirty feet from "the thing", when Vaughan [another policeman] came running towards me at high speed. . . . At that moment there was a very loud swishing noise, as if a plane were diving with the engine cut off – or like a gigantic fuse burning. It lasted about three or four seconds. . . . Realizing that I would have to turn right about before I could start running, I crouched down in what is known as prone-falling position number one. . . . My head was watching, and before I could reach position number two and lie down flat the thing in the road exploded. I had a momentary glimpse of a large ball of blinding wild white light and two concentric rings of colour, the inner one lavender and the outer one violet, as I ducked my head. The ball seemed to be about ten to twenty feet high, and was near the lamp post. Several things happened simultaneously. My head was jerked back due to a heavy blow on the dome and rim of the back of my steel helmet, but I do not remember this for, as my head went back, I received a severe blow on my forehead and the bridge of my nose. The blast bent up the front rim of my helmet and knocked it off my head. The explosion made an indescribable noise – something like a colossal growl – and was accompanied by a veritable tornado of air blast. I felt an excruciating pain in my ears and all sounds were replaced by a very loud singing noise, which I was told later was when I lost my hearing and had my eardrums perforated. I felt that consciousness was slipping from me, and that moment I heard a clear loud voice shouting: "Don't let yourself go, face up to it – hold on." It rallied me and, summoning all my willpower and energy, I succeeded in forcing myself down into a crouching position on the ground, my feet against the curb behind me and my hands covering my face.'

Successive waves of blast bombarded the BBC man with shrapnel and blew him across the road towards the wall of a building, where he staggered to his feet. 'I looked around and it seemed like a scene from Dante's *Inferno*. The front of the building was lit by a reddish-yellow light; a saloon car was on fire to the left of me and the flames from it were stretching out towards the building, and not upwards. Pieces of brick, masonry and glass seemed to appear on the pavement making, to me, no sound. A few dark huddled bodies were round about, and, right in front of me, were two soldiers: one, some feet from a breach in the wall of the building where a fire seemed to be raging, was propped up against the wall with his arms dangling by him, like a rag doll. The other was nearer, about twelve feet from the burning car; he was sitting up with his knees drawn up and supporting himself by his arms – his trousers had been blown off him. I could see that his legs were bare and that he was wearing short grey underpants. He was alive and conscious.'

By the end of the Blitz high explosives and incendiaries had destroyed 220,000 of London's houses and had rendered another 1.5 million temporarily or permanently uninhabitable. The destruction was not confined to the East End. Acre for acre, Chelsea was one of the most heavily bombed boroughs in Britain, only Holborn, Westminster, Stepney and Shoreditch receiving a higher tonnage of bombs. In other close-knit communities outside London the bombing left no one un-touched. Of Clydebank's 12,000 tenement-like buildings, only seven survived undamaged in the raid of 15 March 1942. Hull was heavily bombed in the spring of that year and by the end of May only 6000 of its 93,000 homes had escaped damage. A visitor recorded the scene:

The most spectacular ruins in Hull are along the banks of the River Hull (a small tributary of the Humber) – particularly to the east side. Here one sees the still smouldering remains of the tall flour mills and stores. Ranks, the largest of all, Spillers, Gillboys, Rishworth, Ingleby and Lofthouse are completely destroyed. Only the CWS and Paul's remain undamaged. The workers from the ruined plants now work in these two. Further east and north-east, the industrial and working-class residential areas have suffered heavily. The huge Reckitts works (blue, starch, polish) are almost com-pletely burnt out, and a large power-station is almost unrecognizable. The gasworks look almost untouched, but Hull was without gas for six weeks after the May raids. Whole streets of working-class houses are down. One of the most impressive bomb-holes is on the Holderness Road. There, there is a crater almost 20 yards across, filled with greenish water, in which planks and barrels are floating. By the side of the crater stands the remainder of the Ritz cinema.

The Blitz saw tragedy, heroism and self-sacrifice in equal measure. Sometimes there was fatal muddle. At the beginning of the Blitz, 450 homeless who had taken refuge in a West Ham Rest Centre were killed by a direct hit as the buses sent to evacuate them were wandering, lost, in another borough. There was the quiet courage of individuals: an en-gineer from the gas company calmly repairing flaming splinter holes 60 feet up on the crown of a gasholder; a young female air-raid warden who always felt 'fear, paralysing fear' in a raid, but still went efficiently about her business; and Lieutenant Davis of the Royal Engineers, who in conditions of extreme peril calmly dug out a UXB from the base of the southwest tower at St Paul's.

There were rumours and false alarms. It was widely believed that Liverpool had been put under martial law after the pounding it received in 'May Week'; individuals stubbornly clung to the wholly illogical belief that you were always safe in a bombed house as 'they never hit the same building twice'. In November 1940 the ARP issued a bulletin warning wardens of diabolical German boobytraps, dropped from their bombers, in the form of handbag-shaped, tartan-coloured sweet tins bearing the

legend 'Lyons' Assorted Toffees' and '*Skotch*'. Any found were to be handed in immediately to the nearest police station. None of these fiendish devices was ever found.

A Chelsea firewatcher named Mallett scoffed when he overheard his colleagues discussing a new German 'terror weapon' – a huge coil spring 'like the inside of a gramophone . . . if you got in the way of the thing, they said that it would either cut your legs off or your head off, or cut you in half.' Shortly afterwards, at the height of a raid on a windy night, 'I heard something come down and go with a dull thud. . . . Then I heard this noise.' It was an eerie scraping metallic noise, coming straight for him, and immediately conjured up visions of the deadly coil spring. In mounting panic Mr Mallett fled down Old Church Street followed by the noise. After several minutes of extreme tension he discovered that his pursuer had been a dustbin lid, set rolling by the blast.

On rare occasions there was an encounter with the enemy. Another Chelsea stalwart, Post Warden Matthews, had his work cut out on the evening of 16–17 April:

'Suddenly somebody called out, "There's another coming!" and I remember looking up and seeing what I thought was another parachute mine

Opposite: Never mind the bombs, 'Dig for Victory'. The scene outside London's Bank station after a heavy raid. *Left:* Keep Smiling Through! Grandma's aspidistra is rescued from the wreckage. *Overleaf:* A London Transport bus which has slid into the crater produced by a direct hit on Balham Tube station on the night of 14 October, 1940. Of the 600 people sheltering in the station, 64 drowned in the flood from shattered water and sewage pipes.

95

Above, left: When the blackout comes, a housewife's fancy turns to rug-making.
Above, right: A dramatic Ministry of Information poster gives unwary motorists a
graphic warning. *Below:* The blackout produced a wide range of ephemera and
commercial spin-offs

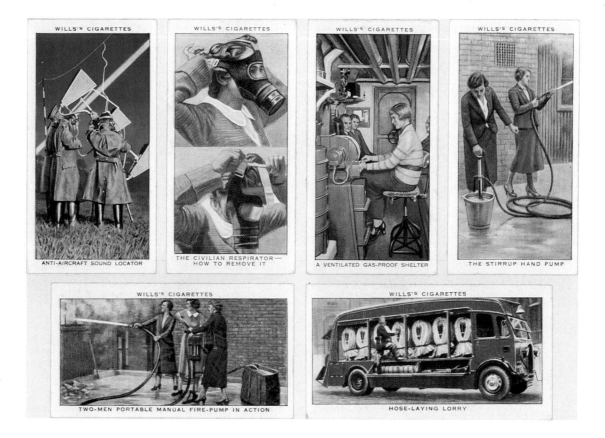

Above: Wills cigarette cards illustrate a number of ARP measures of varying degrees of practicality. *Right:* Advertisers quickly warmed to wartime themes. Throughout the war Guinness was considered good for 'stress' and for 'settling the nerves'

Left: Fry's strove to identify their cocoa with the devil-may-care pilots of the RAF, although one suspects that the airmen's preference was for something just a little bit stronger. Many wartime advertisements contained the depressing reminder that the product in question would only be available when the war was over; the words 'pre-war quality' conjured up visions of a vanished world of consumer affluence. In the meantime, people had to 'Make Do and Mend'. *Below:* A variation on the 'Dig for Victory' theme. During the war years the acreage under the plough in Britain nearly doubled

BETTER THAN EVER KNITTING THIS MONTH

WOMAN and HOME

and GOOD NEEDLEWORK Magazine

9ᵈ

JULY
1942

Left: Woman and Home magazine offers its readers a feast of jam-making. In the fruit season the housewife could take part of the family's jam ration in the form of sugar for making her own preserves. *Above:* Joining the domestic warriors of the Kitchen Front were the irrepressible Cockney comedians Gert and Daisy

Right: Members of the ATS manning a sound-locator. Women played a vital role in AA Command. Training for mixed anti-aircraft batteries began in the spring of 1940, and by the autumn of 1941 women were serving alongside men on gun-sites. The officer commanding the first mixed battery to bring down a German aircraft commented: 'As an old soldier, if I were offered the choice of commanding a mixed battery or a male battery, I say without hesitation I would take the mixed battery. The girls cannot be beaten in action, and in my opinion they are definitely better than the men on the instruments they are manning. Beyond a little natural excitement which only shows itself in rather humorous and quaint remarks, they are quite as steady if not steadier than the men. They are amazingly keen at going into action, and although they are not supposed to learn to use the rifle, they are as keen as anything to do so'. *Below:* Women seamen of the British Overseas Airways Corporation moor a Boeing flying-boat in the summer of 1943. Women seamen were employed by BOAC to operate the launches plying in harbour to service the flying-boats which flew on transatlantic routes and to West Africa and Lisbon

Above: Seaside mortar practice for
factory workers. The broad grins
and mock alarm suggest a certain
amount of staging for the camera

Below: The ironically named 'beauty parlour' at a Royal Ordnance Factory making shells, November 1943. Women workers apply a special cream to their faces to serve as a mask and prevent the skin from absorbing toxic explosive powders. Safety precautions included magazine suits of fire-resistant serge, rubber-soled shoes and fireproof cotton turbans. *Right:* A riot of colour in a parachute-making workshop, May 1943. Each worker fashioned a parachute from 80 yards of fabric

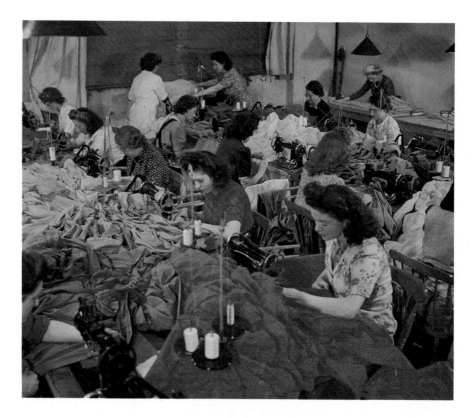

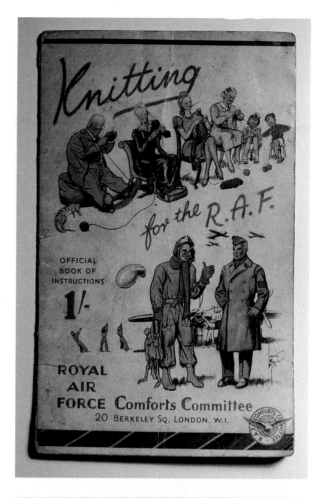

Right: The dance band of the ATS. Most branches of the services encouraged professional musicians in their ranks to form bands. One of the most famous was the Royal Air Force No. I Dance Band, the legendary Squadronnaires, formed when eight members of the Ambrose Orchestra, including Vera Lynn's future husband Harry Lewis, joined the RAF. *Below:* A feast of fun promised by an advertisement for ENSA. *Opposite, top:* An Afternoon Show by an ENSA Company in a NAAFI Canteen Hut, 1941, by Frank Graves. *Opposite, bottom:* Foreign Servicemen in Hyde Park: Early Summer, 1940, by Kenneth Rowntree

Left: An air gunner of the US Eighth Air Force. By January 1943 the 'Mighty Eighth' had over 500 bombers stationed in the United Kingdom. By May 1944 it was strong enough to despatch its first 1,000-bomber raid against the Third Reich. *Below:* The Operations Room at Bomber Command HQ, High Wycombe, by Charles Cundall

Above: Australian bomber crews celebrate a Lancaster's 100th mission. The aircraft displays a redundant boast by Hermann Goering. In the autumn of 1944 the strategic air offensive was moving towards its climax. During this period Bomber Command alone dropped more bombs on Germany than it had during the entire course of 1943

Overleaf: Crowds stream past the Cenotaph in Whitehall on VE-Day while more intrepid souls view the proceedings from the roof of a Ministry building

Some souvenirs of VE-Day

coming down. It was absolutely terrifying. You couldn't look away from the thing, and there you were, just trying to make yourself as small as possible in the debris. And I suddenly realized it wasn't a mine, it was a man, it was an airman on the end of this parachute, and he dropped down quite fast over the roadway and down on the foreshore of the river, on the [Chelsea] embankment. A number of us rushed across there and then we looked rather cautiously over the wall. We had ideas about paratroop invasions. I remember a couple of firemen training a hose and I was clutching my axe and I expect everybody else was wondering what we could do if the man turned a gun on us, but someone went down the steps which are just a little way along the embankment there, and got hold of him. . . . He was a youngster I should think in his early twenties. I remember he was wearing a green flying suit and he was pretty well the same colour himself. He was very correct in his behaviour – he didn't say anything, he didn't do anything, he just stood more or less at attention. I remember feeling his arm quite rigid when I got hold of him, and then something rather surprising happened. . . . Somebody rushed and kicked him in the seat, very hard. I suppose it was somebody who'd had someone killed or was just overcome by the strain of events, but anyway he, the man who kicked him, then rushed round to the front of him and succeeded in getting a pistol out of the pocket in front of his flying suit, and anyway, somebody else took the pistol from the little man, I don't know what he'd have done if he hadn't wrested it away from him. Then a War Reserve policeman came along at that point, and shortly afterwards another one, and I remember seeing them marching this German airman off along the embankment just as if he'd been drunk and disorderly on a Saturday night.'

This story captures the fear, the relief at survival and the fatigue which were felt by all who lived through the Blitz. Lack of sleep was high on the list of complaints and a godsend to the manufacturers of Horlicks, whose advertisements promised that a cup of the milky drink last thing at night 'will help you take the second year of the war in your stride'.

Londoners took their Horlicks and the bombing; 'London can take it' was the popular phrase of the day, as the citizens of the capital gritted their teeth and carried on. Contrary to all expectations, the Blitz saw a wholesale decline in neurotic disorders. People seemed to be able to cope with the bombs rather better than they handled the stresses and strains of peacetime city life. There were fewer suicides and the figures for drunkenness dropped by 50 per cent. On occasions, however, the bottle proved a welcome distraction from the bombs. Angus Calder tells the story of one woman whose nightly air-raid precautions consisted of happily drinking herself into a state of insensibility. At the height of a big raid she was found at the foot of the stairs, having taken a tumble from top to bottom. She was quite unharmed by the experience and was slumbering peacefully while the barrage raged all around.

Those who remained more alert became increasingly sensitive to the imminence of danger. The film director Paul Rotha noted: 'As time goes on you get experienced. A plane overhead, a scream, you count one – two – three – four, they either get closer or get distant. If closer, you seek handy shelter – a doorway usually. If distant, you go on doing what you're doing. . . . It's remarkable how sensitive your ears get.'

Doggedly the overwhelming majority of people continued to turn up for work, often travelling by lorries standing in for 'blitzed' buses. Mary Benney, a young worker in an aircraft factory in the London area, recalled, 'There was very little absenteeism caused by the raids; in part because we all felt that the raids gave an added importance to our work,

Above: A recruiting poster for the Auxiliary Fire Service. During the war 793 firemen and 25 firewomen lost their lives while 7,000 sustained serious injuries. Many more were temporarily blinded by heat or sparks, and all who joined the Service were affected by the strain of working long hours in conditions of great danger without sleep or regular meals. It was not until the end of the Blitz, in May 1941, that Herbert Morrison, the Minister of Home Security, reorganised Britain's complicated patchwork of fire brigades into the National Fire Service.

but much more because we knew that if we didn't turn up our mates would be worrying. You would see men staggering at their work for lack of sleep, snatching a ten minutes' doze in the canteen over their food, and still, when knocking-off time came, going off with a cheerful, "See yer in the morning, boys!"

'It became a sort of war cry, a common affirmation of faith pregnant with unstated defiances and resolutions, that phrase. We threw it at each other gaily, but always with the implication very near the surface, "If I don't see yer, it means they'll be digging me out."'

The opening of the Blitz had temporarily closed London's theatres, with the exception of the Windmill, which soldiered on with its inimitable mixture of comedy and striptease and the famous slogan, 'We Never Closed!' By Christmas 1940 the West End was beginning to come back to life, but in the intervening months German bombs had 'closed' a number of theatres, including the Holborn Empire, where Vera Lynn had been starring in the popular revue *Applesauce!* A direct hit made the cast of *Applesauce!* as homeless as many another family until the beginning of March 1941 when the show reopened at the Palladium. Inevitably the raids dictated theatrical routine just as they did the domestic routine of the audiences who flocked to see the show.

Vera Lynn recalls, 'Because of the nightly bombing, the first house went on very early, about 4.15 in the afternoon. The warning siren would usually sound during the mid-evening second house, as often as not at the time I was coming on stage for my spot. There was a sign at the side of the stage which, rather unnecessarily, lit up to say that a raid was in progress, but most of the audience stayed in their seats. I was never thrown out of my stride by bombs falling nearby; you'd take no more notice of a bomb going off than of a drummer falling off his stool. I always felt that if the audience could see us getting on with the job, they would be encouraged to stay and to enjoy the show. On many nights they got an extra helping of entertainment. If the bombs were still falling at the end of the show, we'd have an informal sing-song, with members of the audience getting up on stage. In the lulls people would gradually drift away, leaving the theatre to the cast and the firewatchers. We'd all sit about and make ourselves as comfortable as we could until the all-clear sounded.'

One of the West End's most glittering night spots was the Café de Paris, in Coventry Street, which had reopened at the height of the Blitz. Because it was situated underground, beneath the Rialto Cinema, the Café de Paris was advertised as London's safest restaurant.

On the night of 8 March the Café de Paris was packed with officers on leave and fashionable London society, all bent on forgetting the war. At about a quarter to ten Ken 'Snakehips' Johnson and his Caribbean band were launching themselves into 'Oh, Johnny' when two bombs plunged through the Rialto's roof straight into the Café de Paris. Thirty-four died, including Johnson and another member of the band, and sixty were seriously wounded. Only one bomb exploded; the other burst open on impact, spewing its rank-smelling yellow contents over the dead and the dying.

One of those who survived was Ulric Huggins, an officer in the Royal Navy. Seconds before the bombs struck he had been drinking champagne. 'The first impression I got was of darkness and dust, and I noticed the champagne bottle lying horizontally on the table. My first instinct at that moment was to pick it up and put it upright. It must have been a matter of some seconds afterwards that I remember I stood up, with the champagne bottle still in my hand, and poured out drinks for the other

three people at the table. And a memory I have very clearly is that, as the champagne rose in the glasses, which incidentally were standing upright on the table unbroken, the foam on the top was grey with dust. And I remember quite clearly wiping the foam off with my finger before I drank. And then I turned round, and there at my feet was the waiter who had been leaning over me pouring the champagne – dead, of course.'

The rescue workers arrived amid scenes of macabre horror. One woman recalled having her broken leg bathed in champagne. Another, sprawled wounded and semi-conscious across the corpse of a kilted Highland officer, felt a looter slipping the rings off her fingers. In contrast, another woman, Miss Irene Ballyn, remembered helping a wounded RAF officer to the ladies' cloakroom. Here she bathed his hand, which was missing one of its fingers, under the cold tap. Suddenly she was overcome with emotion and burst into tears. The officer turned to her and said with infinite concern, 'Don't cry, my dear. It's my hand, not yours.'

By April 1941 the big clean-up was under way. In London 16,000 repairers were at work, and by the end of the month they had made over a million damaged homes wind and weatherproof. That summer *Housewife* magazine ran a brisk article on how a London housewife had set about clearing away the mess after a near miss:

Sifting through the debris at the Café de Paris after it was hit on the night of 8 March, 1941.

99

When dawn broke and crept through our rafters, showing itself between the plasterless laths of the ceilings, we shook ourselves, stretched cramped limbs and took stock of the situation. . . . The time was 5.30 a.m. . . . We concentrated our own forces on the dining room–sitting room first, and then worked solidly through the house together. . . . First we picked up the larger bits of ceiling and glass and threw them through the window. Everything went through the window, whether debris, to be swept into heaps later, or rugs to be beaten. . . . The kitchen . . . was an indescribable mess. Even in the cupboards the uncovered food was full of glass splinters, the sink was full of wet grime, the table and floor thick with debris. Even the covered food, on inspection, too often revealed those bright specks. . . . We rolled up the mats and threw them out and swept the entire floor, as well as everything else that would sweep, including tops of cupboards. Where things were scrubbable we scrubbed. The steam from the hot water tap rose like a blessing on our labours. There was plenty of fresh air, and we began to sing. The lawn outside was full of mats, the air beyond full of bangs and clashings of glass as neighbours toiled with their own blasted properties. They, and a host of workmen, walked freely in and out, demanding milk, hot water, and a wash-and-brush-up. . . . Incidentally we realized how very difficult it is to safeguard food. Locked cupboards fly open, tops fly off, tins are riven through, heavy boxes smash open. On the other hand, fragile things often escape. Our pan of last year's preserved eggs survived their second land mine successfully. . . . We worked ferociously through the house all that morning till the early afternoon. By four o'clock we could sit down in the midst of our labours and say they were good. . . . Shocks bring a temporary surge of reactionary energy. You have to cash in on that at once before it goes on the ebb. If you can do this you can handle a major catastrophe (or what would have seemed like one once) in terms of routine.

The long road back had begun.

Opposite: The capricious legacy of the bombs. One half of the street a pile of dust, the other virtually untouched.

Right: Broad grins for the camera as the bedding is retrieved from bomb-damaged homes.

Far left: The man with the big cigar. Winston Churchill inspects coastal defences in the North-East in 1942. *Inset:* Touring Bristol during the Blitz. In October 1940 he told the House of Commons: 'We must be united, we must be undaunted, we must be inflexible. Our qualities and deeds must burn and gleam through the gloom of Europe until they become the veritable beacons of its salvation'.

Above: Churchill and the generals. The Prime Minister inspects the 'dragon's teeth' of the German Siegfried Line in March 1945. With him are Field Marshal Brooke (extreme left), Chief of the Imperial General Staff, and Field Marshal Montgomery (second left), commander of 21st Army Group. *Left:* The moment of triumph – Churchill is mobbed by crowds in Whitehall on VE-Day. *Below:* Even when photographed from behind, Churchill radiates pugnacity as he watches a Short Stirling of Bomber Command.

6

AUSTERITY BRITAIN

National self-sufficiency was the keynote of the Home Front.

All kinds of songs and jingles run through my head from time to time, reminding me of the wartime days of rationing and salvage drives. If you lived through those times you'll remember this one:

> *Hey! Little Hen! When, when, when*
> *Will you lay an egg for my tea?*
> *Hey! Little Hen! When, when, when*
> *Will you try to supply one for me?*

Eggs were in short supply during the war, although no one worried much about salmonella then – it sounds more like something that was in cans, 'on points' and in short supply than a deadly disease. For much of the time we made do with dried eggs. The strutting hen in the Ministry of Food advertisements assured us that 'Dried eggs are my eggs, my whole eggs and nothing but my eggs', but a dried egg omelette left one with a few lingering doubts. Tommy Handley offered his radio audience his own inimitable variety of eggs which were 'all singing, all humming and all bumen. The only eggs that are all they're cracked up to be. . . . With every dozen we give away a gas mask. "ITMA" eggs can be whipped but they can't be beaten!'

Imported fruits like bananas disappeared altogether. In the winter of 1944 I returned from a tour of duty with ENSA on the Arakan Front in Burma. Taking pride of place among my souvenirs was a large bunch of bananas, an almost unknown sight in wartime Britain. There was a young mother standing on the railway station with her small son. She kept eyeing the bananas in disbelief and finally plucked up courage to come and ask me if she could have one for her little boy, as he had never tasted one. I am afraid the result of the tasting was an anticlimax as he spat it out and said "argah"; in other words he hated it. His introduction to this forbidden wartime fruit had been an unmitigated disaster. The same scene was to be repeated across the country after the war, when anxious mothers treated their tots to their first banana!

One of the great battle cries on the Home Front was 'Dig for Victory!':

> *Dig! Dig! Dig! And your muscles will grow big,*
> *Keep on pushing the spade!*
> *Don't mind the worms,*
> *Just ignore their squirms,*
> *And when your back aches laugh with glee*
> *And keep on diggin'*
> *Till we give our foes a wiggin'*
> *Dig!Dig!Dig! to victory.*

Britain had to be self-sufficient, and every spare patch of ground was turned over to cultivation. In Hyde Park there were allotments in the shadow of the Albert Memorial. Rationing produced its frustrations,

The demonstration allotments in Hyde Park transform the familiar view of the Albert Memorial. In the drive to 'Dig for Victory', a slogan coined in 1939, even golf courses were dug up and back gardens came to resemble miniature farms, crammed with chicken runs and rabbit hutches. The cluck of hens was heard in some of London's most fashionable residential quarters.

but it meant that the nation as a whole was much better fed than it had been in the 1930s and, I suspect, than it is now. As part of the war effort people were bombarded with information on the most economical and nutritious ways to use their rationed, and unrationed, food. Potatoes, which were unrationed, featured heavily in our diet. There was even a Christmas Potato Fair in 1942, held on a bomb site in Oxford Street; each visitor signed a pledge: 'I promise as my Christmas gift to sailors who have to bring our bread that I will do all I can to eat home-grown potatoes.'

I played a small part in the food campaign. A Manchester newspaper printed one of my recipes which reflects the shortages with which the wartime housewife fought a daily battle:

Oranges are now obtainable; unfortunately jellies are not, but a very few people may have a jelly. For those who have not, gelatine may be used in place of the jelly.

For my favourite sweet – orange jelly – you want one orange jelly or a good half ounce of gelatine, ½ pint of water, ½ pint of orange juice, the rind of four oranges, and sugar to taste.

With a potato peeler take the rind from the oranges, put into the water and bring to boiling point. Allow to simmer for ten minutes. Strain and add the jelly, or the gelatine softened in a very little cold water. This should be dissolved thoroughly in the hot water, but do not let it boil.

Sweeten to taste, add the strained orange juice and, if necessary, stir in a little more castor sugar if you are making it with the gelatine.

Allow to set and serve with custard.

An orange, quartered and arranged in the jelly before it sets, makes it look very pretty.

In March 1941 a chemist's shop in Southampton displayed this sign in its window:

We regret we are unable to supply

Vacuum flasks	Rolls Razors
Saccharines	Rolls razor blades
Lipsticks	Gillette razor blades
Rouges	7 O'clock razor blades
All tubes of vanishing cream	Brushless shaving cream
All barley sugar sweets	Nivea cream

Until notice removed

Shortages and rationing provide one of the major themes of life on the Home Front and with it images of ration cards, endless queues, 'utility' clothes and the dubious culinary delights of whale meat and Woolton pie. The shortages were no less exasperating for being inevitable – 'There's a war on, you know,' was the automatic response to every complaint. But rationing was widely welcomed when it was introduced and helped to win the war. As a Ministry of Food advertisement boasted:

> *Because of the pail, the scraps were saved,*
> *Because of the scraps, the pigs were saved,*
> *Because of the pigs, the rations were saved,*
> *Because of the rations, the ships were saved,*
> *Because of the ships, the island was saved,*
> *Because of the island, the Empire was saved,*
> *And all because of a housewife's pail.*

In the First World War rationing had been introduced only in 1918. Ration cards had been prepared in 1938 and issued in September 1939, but the Chamberlain government dithered over the immediate implementation of the scheme. This was another indication of its remoteness from the general public, who were not only reconciled to the idea of rationing but wanted it to be introduced as soon as possible. People preferred equality to a free for all in which the well-off would stockpile food and the poor go hungry. This widespread feeling was summed up by an East End grocer, who complained that the failure to introduce rationing was 'bringing in all the rich people from the West End to take the poor people's food. I came back from lunch this morning and found a beautiful car outside. A lady and her husband were carrying twenty-eight pounds [of sugar] each – and the chauffeur twenty-eight pounds on each arm. I made them put it all back again and gave them three pounds each. I don't think that sort of thing is right – they take all the poor people's food. They don't give the poor a chance.'

Opposed to the introduction of rationing were Winston Churchill,

Opposite: A Gallup poll of November 1939 revealed that six out of ten favoured food rationing. In April 1943 *The Lady* magazine summed up most people's feelings: 'An overwhelming majority of women of all classes are thankful for the food controls and praise their efficient running. Many wives and mothers are able to give their families better and more regular meals under war conditions than ever before.'

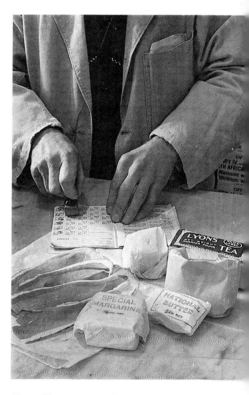

Above: The ration card, the most important single item in every housewife's life.

then First Lord of the Admiralty, and the *Daily Express*, which thundered:

> The public should revolt against the food rationing system, that dreadful and terrible inequity which some ministers want to adopt. There is no necessity for the trouble and expense of rationing because there may be shortages of this or that inessential commodity. Why should old women be forced to wait here and there before the shops for their supplies? This form of folly is difficult and almost impossible to understand.

The *Daily Express* was marching resolutely out of step with public opinion, and on Monday, 8 January, the ration book became the single most important item in the life of every housewife. The first foodstuffs to be rationed were sugar, butter, ham and bacon, although the bacon ration, at 8 oz a week, was initially fixed at a level higher than the average pre-war consumption. In March meat was rationed, by price rather than by weight. Each person over the age of six was entitled to 1s 10d worth of meat per week, while the under-sixes were allotted 11d worth; offal was not rationed. July saw the introduction of tea rationing. Clearly things were getting serious.

In the autumn of 1940 heavy shipping losses in the Battle of the Atlantic were threatening Britain's supply lifeline. By the beginning of 1942 food imports were running at less than half their pre-war level, and the tide of Japanese conquest in the Far East was shortly to cut off important sources of rice, sugar and tea. Rationing was no longer a 'folly' but a fact of national survival. It had been extended to include preserves (jam, margarine, syrups and treacle), sweets and cooking fat. In May 1941 cheese was rationed for the first time, initially at the miserly rate of 1 oz a week. A month later shell eggs were embraced by a system of controlled distribution which provided adults with an average of about 30 eggs a year.

In November 1941 a 'points' system was applied to canned meat, fish and vegetables, which enabled the consumer to choose between a range of goods, each with a fixed points price. Under the points system an individual received 20 points for four weeks, a measure which did much to prevent the hoarding of tinned goods by the well-to-do. In January 1942 the points system was extended to dried fruit, rice, tapioca and pulses; in February canned fruit, tomatoes and peas were added to the list; in April it was the turn of condensed milk and breakfast cereals; in July syrup and treacle; in August biscuits; and in December oat flakes and rolled oats.

Great ingenuity was now required to assemble the ingredients for a celebratory meal. It was a major operation to prepare a birthday cake, as Rosemary Moonen recalled: 'My twenty-first birthday cake was a wow! It was 1942, and we had difficulty in saving our points for both dried fruit and tinned meat for the party. So we compromised and used soaked prunes and a few sultanas. The result was somewhat heavy, but filling. Icing sugar was scarce and eggs even scarcer, so we made a type of chocolate frosting with cocoa, icing sugar, one egg white and water. We found some candles, but had no icing sugar or forcing-bag rosette nozzle to write on or decorate the cake. So I had a brainwave. I cut the end off an empty toothpaste tube and filled it with condensed milk! With this I adorned the cake – 'Happy 21st Birthday' – and to my relief it didn't run too much! However, with our meagre points to provide sandwiches and our 'Prune and Condensed Milk Cake', we managed to feed around thirty guests and have a wonderful party. The cake was demolished with relish!'

In August 1942 an adult's meat ration was fixed at 1s 2d a week, covering beef, veal, mutton and pork but not rabbit or poultry. This translated into approximately 1 lb meat per person per week; children under six were entitled to 7d worth a week. Both adults and children were limited to 4 oz bacon and ham a week, 8 oz sugar, 8 oz fat (of which 4 oz had to be margarine) and 8 oz cheese. Over the period of a month the consumer was entitled to buy 16 oz jam, marmalade or mincemeat; in the fruit season the housewife could take part of the family's jam ration in the form of sugar for making her own preserves. Over the same period the sweet ration was 8 oz. Over eight weeks the holder of an adult ration card was entitled to a single packet of dried eggs (imported in huge quantities from the United States under the terms of Lend-Lease), which was the equivalent of a dozen eggs in shell; the allowance for children under six was two packets.

Fish was not rationed; nor were potatoes and bread, which became the principal bulk items in the national diet. White bread vanished in the autumn of 1942 to be replaced by the nutritious but lumpy 'national wheatmeal loaf', made from flour of 85 per cent extraction. The national loaf was universally unpopular. The story goes that Ernest Bevin, the Minister of Labour, complained about it to Clement Attlee, Churchill's Deputy Prime Minister, claiming that it was indigestible. 'I can't digest the stuff in the middle – I throw it away, it's just waste.' At this point Bevin belched loudly, adding with an air of triumph, 'There you are – what did I tell you?'

Throwing away bread was not encouraged by the Ministry of Food, whose anti-waste campaign occasionally led to some unusual prosecutions. On 20 January 1943 the readers of the *Bristol Evening Post* were treated to this item:

Bread Wasted

Miss Mary Bridget O'Sullivan, Normandy Avenue, Barnet, Herts, was fined a total of ten pounds, with two guineas costs, at Barnet today for permitting bread to be wasted. Her servant, Miss Domenica Rosa Persi, was fined five shillings for wasting bread.

It was stated that the servant was twice seen throwing bread to birds in the garden, and when Miss O'Sullivan was interviewed she admitted that bread was put out every day. 'I cannot see the birds starve,' she said.

Rationing produced a monotonous diet but one that was shared as equitably and efficiently as possible across the nation. Inevitably the application of the system across the board led to winners and losers. People who lived alone fared less well than large families, who could pool their resources to make the most of what was available. Heavy workers in industry needed more calories per day than the national average of about 3000 which was considered sufficient for moderately active adults.

Many people made up the gap by cultivating allotments, the number of which increased from 815,000 in 1939 to nearly 1.5 million in 1943. Others installed a chicken coop in their gardens, to such good effect that by 1944 domestic hen keepers were producing a quarter of the nation's supply of fresh eggs. Pig-keeping was another aspect of wartime animal husbandry, and by 1945 there were nearly 7000 'Pig Clubs', rearing their porkers on kitchen waste.

By 1943 the nation was better nourished than it had been in the 1930s. Milk and vegetable consumption was up by 30 per cent, while meat consumption had fallen by 20 per cent. The emphasis was on nutrition content rather than variety, the 'building bricks of protein' extolled by

Right: The members of a pig club proudly display their porker. For those who could not afford bacon, there was a substitute, called 'macon', which was really made out of mutton. *Opposite:* Health care for wartime babies at a Hatfield nursery in 1943. Wartime planning and social provision, and the practical benefits which flowed from them, had an important impact on ordinary people's lives. Nevertheless, new mothers had to cope with a shortage of prams, push-chairs, baby baths and rubber teats, and the problems caused by fathers absent in the forces and unsettled homes.

Charles Hill, the Radio Doctor. Oranges, for example, were an extremely rare commodity, and bananas disappeared altogether. There is an amusing moment at the beginning of the Launder and Gilliat film *Millions Like Us* (1943) when a subtitle flashes on the screen to remind the audience that an orange is 'a spherical pulpish fruit of reddish-brown colour'.

Rationing and its associated provisions for priority groups also had important social effects. Free school meals for the children of poorer families, free cod-liver oil and orange juice for the under-twos, and extra eggs and milk for expectant mothers, were important additions to the diet of the needy.

By 1944 the average housewife was spending 11s of every £1 on rationed food and 2s more on points-rationed items. The points system allowed for an element of choice, but there was no choice over where she shopped for her rationed foods. Each shopkeeper's supplies were tied to the number of his registered customers. You presented him with your ration book and he cancelled the coupons received for specific foods. Favoured customers often received special treatment from 'under the counter'. Mrs Clara Milburn, a middle-class housewife who lived near Coventry, wrote in her diary in 1944:

> A nice bright morning, sun shining out of a cloudless blue sky at 8 a.m. Later lovely billowy clouds formed and unfortunately a wind sprang up – just as if everything was not dry as dust already. The beautiful car bustled to the butcher and then Twink [her dog] and I walked on our six feet to the grocer, where we picked up one or two unexpected oddments. One was a pound of suet! It's extraordinary how there's never a mite of suet in the winter, but in the middle of summer out comes a packet of 'Cook's Suet' from under the counter! Then three tomatoes were put in a bag surreptitiously and placed quickly in my basket.

For others food – or rather the lack of it – could become an obsession. Joan Ierston's work as a Land Girl encouraged a healthy appetite which her landlady failed signally to satisfy:

Right: Cigarettes were in permanent short supply throughout the war. Favoured customers could take advantage of 'under the counter' stock. *Below:* A Churchillian reminder to watch waste in the kitchen. The war led to some remarkable culinary improvisations. On the 'Kitchen Front' radio programme S. B. Mais asked listeners: 'Have you tried cabbage tops, swede tops and radish tops cooked as greens, or the fronds of young bracken, which tastes like asparagus? You don't want to be too cranky, but you do want to use what's handy . . . even if you've never tried it before.'

In my first digs the landlady never cooked a second vegetable, except on Sunday; we had cold meat on Monday, and sausage for the rest of the week. Sometimes she cooked potatoes with the sausage, but often she left us a slice of bread each. The two sausages on a large, cold, green glass plate greeted us on our return from a day on leeks or sprouts and a three-mile cycle ride each way. My friend combated the gloom with a small bottle of whisky which had been given to her and which she hid behind the curtain until dire need arose. A neighbour once brought round a sack of carrots, which he said were for the rabbit, but we benefited from this act of kindness. . . . At the hostel we had dried egg once a week for breakfast, but the good lady in charge like to cook it overnight, so it resembled, and tasted like, sawdust on toast. We had fish paste on toast too some mornings, which brought forth rude remarks. . . .

Presiding over the dried egg mountain and the serried ranks of the National Wheatmeal Loaf was Lord Woolton, the Minister of Food from April 1940 to December 1943. His Ministry was a vast bureaucracy which employed 50,000 civil servants and operated over 1000 local Food Offices, its front line in the rationing war. The Ministry was nothing less than 'the biggest shop in the world' – the sole importer of basic foodstuffs and the sole buyer of domestically produced fatstock and milk. Either directly or indirectly (through government-sponsored committees of formerly independent producers and distributors) the Ministry controlled the production and distribution of virtually all foods in the United Kingdom.

To this potentially faceless and forbidding government machine Lord Woolton brought an endearingly human touch. He had begun his career as a social worker in the slums before rising to the chairmanship of a chain of department stores, a background which enabled him to blend a business and administrative flair with a genuine concern for the poorest members of society. He was also a considerable propagandist, and it was with an infectious enthusiasm that he threw himself into the task of selling the benefits of rationing to the British public and educating it into better eating habits.

An ebullient communicator and shrewd handler of the media, Woolton bombarded the public with improving information. Cinema-goers were treated to soap-opera style 'food flashes' between feature films; radio listeners tuned in to the five-minute 'Kitchen Front', broadcast every day at 8.15 a.m.; newspapers and magazines were peppered with Ministry-approved cookery columns and advertisements proffering advice on everything from Christmas puddings without eggs to the legendary Woolton pie. Sadly, in spite of the universal admiration accorded the tireless Lord Woolton, the vegetable pie which bore his name never really caught on with the public.

Carrots, which were seldom in short supply, were the subject of a flood of resistible suggestions from the Ministry. One of the more optimistic was for carrot marmalade. In his memoirs of a wartime childhood Derek Lambert recalled a brief encounter with this novel preserve. His mother was an assiduous collector of the Ministry of Food's leaflets:

> In one of these ... she found a recipe for carrot marmalade. Dessert oranges were a rarity, Sevilles were nonexistent.
>
> From the garden where, in the chalk-diced earth, carrot flies were nurtured more readily than carrots, she gathered a withered harvest. The carrots were boiled and sweetened, the scum, thick with carrot fly corpses, removed and the residue sealed in jam jars.
>
> One morning a jar was put on the breakfast table with supreme nonchalance. Only those accustomed to the prelude to one of my mother's wartime offerings would have recognized the symptoms: stertorous breathing, high colour, an exaggerated indifference to our reactions.
>
> My father, an undemonstrative man, spread the nectar on his bread and bit into it. He frowned and said: 'What was that?'
>
> 'Carrot marmalade,' said my mother.
>
> With unusual deliberation – I have since pondered on the tyrannical undertones – he picked up the jar, took it into the garden and poured it on the compost heap.

The great wartime increase in communal eating partly compensated for the limitations of rationing. The number of industrial factory canteens leapt from about 1500 in 1939 to 18,500 in 1944. They received an extra allowance of meat, cheese, butter and sugar per meal – approximately twice the norm for heavy workers – which did much to close the calorie gap.

Good, cheap and plentiful food was provided by the chain of self-service British Restaurants, run by local authorities and subsidized by central government. By September 1943 there were over 2000 British Restaurants serving 600,000 meals a day at about 1s a head. Labour-saving self-service methods were quickly copied by commercial caterers. This way of eating out was a novelty for many fastidious members of the middle class, as Mrs Milburn revealed in a diary entry of April 1943:

> A dash round the house this morning, *very cross* having received the —— petrol officer's refusal to grant even our modest amount of petrol, after further application. Mrs Gorton called for me at 10.45 a.m. and, with Mrs Curtis (and we later picked up her son, the parson here), we were soon at

Opposite, below: One of the more engaging dietary myths of the war. In 1940, in Britain's darkest hour, a committee of nutritionists devised the 'Basal Diet', which estimated that, if the worst came to the worst, the average Briton could survive on a basic daily ration of 12oz of bread, 1lb of potatoes, 2oz of oatmeal, 1oz of fats, 6oz of vegetables and 6/10 of a pint of milk. This drastic diet was never introduced, but the emphasis on bread, potatoes and carrots remained.

CARROTS
keep you healthy and help you to see in the blackout

Above: Good food could still be had in wartime London, at a price. *Left:* More typical were restaurants like this one, run by Mrs Staines, in Chilworth Mews. Two wartime constants – bread and uniforms – are much in evidence here. For some unfathomable reason, this photograph, taken for *Illustrated* magazine in April 1943, was banned by the censor. Perhaps the Ministry of Information objected to the sight of people so clearly enjoying themselves in such informal style.

Leamington, myself heartily glad of the lift. It enabled me to shop before going to lunch. All the tables were reserved, so I tried the cafeteria – my first experience of this kind of meal. Even wartime difficulties did not make me enjoy this method of serving oneself: pick up the tray, slide it along the bars, receive a slop of meat (not *too* bad, but a bit gristly), far too much potato and gravy and masses of cabbage. Next three prunes and a half and not too bad custard. With these I paid the woman at the end, who spoke in whispers, and walked off to a table – to find I had forgotten my knife and fork, etc. – went back and got them and ate. The coffee was vile, so I left it. Last week I had an excellent meal in the room below for a few coppers more!

There was a huge increase in eating out during the war, not least because of the call-up of women for war work. Before the war the twelve restaurants in the Granada cinema chain employed three chefs and seventy-five female staff, who produced 250,000 meals a year. During the war, with rationing at its peak and the number of restaurants reduced to nine, Granada's sixteen chefs and 200 female staff turned out 1.5 million meals a year. The rigours of rationing produced some remarkable menus in Granada's Scottish restaurants, whose bills of fare boasted gulls' eggs, venison sausages, rooks, lobster and on one memorable occasion 'Roast Eagle and Two Veg'.

In commercial restaurants customers were limited to one main course and a maximum charge of 5s. The maximum charge was eventually lifted for 'superior' restaurants, a measure which produced a host of sharp practices and colossal bills. The Conservative MP Sir Henry 'Chips' Channon noted in his diary that a lunch at Claridges for three had set him back £10.

If you had the money and the contacts you could still eat in pre-war style. Fortnum and Mason's shelves were groaning with unrationed luxury items, at a price. In his novel *Unconditional Surrender* Evelyn Waugh painted a vivid picture of an exclusive restaurant in ration-bound wartime London:

Sustaining fare at the works canteen. The nation itself was sustained by massive quantities of food supplied by the United States under the terms of Lend-Lease. In September 1941 alone this included some 15,000 long tons of beans, 18,000 of evaporated milk, 40,000 of oranges, 50,000 of canned fruit and 15,000 of prunes. At the height of the war the United States was meeting nearly one-third of Britain's food requirements.

In a famine-stricken world the little fish restaurant dispensed in their seasons Colchester oysters, Scotch salmon, lobsters, prawns . . . and often caviar, obtained, only Ruben knew how, through diplomatic channels. Most surprising of all there sometimes appeared cheeses from France, collected by intrepid parachutists and conveyed home by submarine. There was an abundance of good wine, enormously costly, at a time when the cellars of hotels were empty and wine merchants dealt out meagre monthly parcels only to their oldest customers. Ruben had for some years enjoyed a small and appreciative clientele. . . . There was also an increasing dilution of odd-looking men who called the proprietor 'Mr Ruben' and carried large quantities of bank notes in their hip pockets. That restaurant was a rare candle in a dark and naughty world. Kerstie Kilbannock, who had made noxious experiments with custard powder and condiments, once asked: 'Do tell me, Ruben, how do you make your mayonnaise?' and received the grave reply: 'Quite simply, my lady, fresh eggs and olive oil.'

On 7 March 1944 life imitated art when 'Chips' Channon gave a dinner party at his London home: 'There was gaiety, *Stimmung*, even some drunkenness. The food was good – oysters, salmon, dressed crab, minced chicken, etc. I counted nineteen cars outside my house. No raids disturbed our revels and we all wished that Hitler could have seen so luxurious a festival in London at the height of the war.'

Above: Berketex Utility fashions by Norman Hartnell. In 1943 a woman might spend under £5 for a well-designed Utility suit. *Below:* wartime shopping at Selfridges.

However shameless, this kind of self-indulgence in the middle of sacrifice was both rare and statistically irrelevant. 'Chips' Channon might scoff his salmon but far more important was the fact that the children of the poor received their free milk.

Clothes rationing, based on the points system, was introduced in June 1941. Once again Churchill was firmly opposed to this step, protesting that it would 'strip the nation to the buff'. According to Oliver Lyttelton, then the President of the Board of Trade, the Prime Minister's objections were cunningly overcome by two members of the Cabinet who tackled him on clothes rationing in May 1941 when he was engrossed in the hunt for the German pocket battleship *Bismarck*. 'Do what you like,' growled Churchill, 'but please don't bother me now!'

At first the clothes ration was intended to provide one complete outfit a year, with women enjoying some freedom of choice over accessories. But in the spring of 1942 the ration was cut from 66 coupons a year to 60 coupons over 15 months (manual workers were allowed an extra 10 coupons a year for working clothes). This did not go very far. Unless he chose to blow them all at once, they would enable a man to buy one pair of socks every four months, one pair of shoes every eight months, one shirt every twenty months, one vest and one pair of pants every two years, one pair of trousers and one jacket every two years, one waistcoat every five years and one overcoat every seven years, leaving three coupons for items like handkerchiefs.

The better-off benefited from the points rationing of clothes. Not only did they already have well-stocked wardrobes, but they were also able to make modest additions of good-quality clothes which 'cost' the same number of points as the shoddily made garments which clothed the poor. However, the points system allowed the Board of Trade to encourage the sale of particular garments by reducing their points value or check a rush by raising the value.

On 19 March 1942 the readers of *The Times* were informed of the Board of Trade's plans to save valuable material:

From May 1st all men's and youth's jackets, waistcoats and trousers will be subject to the following restrictions:

Jackets. No double-breasted jackets; not more than three pockets, no slits or buttons on cuffs; not more than three buttons on front; no patch pockets; no half belt, no fancy belts and no metal or leather buttons.

Waistcoats. Plain, single-breasted only, no collar; not more than two pockets; not more than five buttons; no back straps and no chain hole.

Trousers. Maximum width of trouser bottoms 19 inches, plain bottoms – no permanent turn-ups; not more than three pockets; no side or back straps; no extension waistbands; no pleats; no elastic in waistbands.

General. No zip fasteners, and no raised seams.

The same principal of cutting out unnecessary frills was applied to the 'Utility' clothes, introduced in 1942, which were rigorously controlled in price and material. Top names in the fashion world were commissioned to design a range of practical and attractive women's utility clothes which was hailed by the journalist Anne Scott-James as a 'fashion revolution': 'They are excellent clothes at government-controlled prices. They cut out luxury and defeat the profiteer. Don't be misled by the term "utility clothes". They have nothing to do with boiler suits and gum-boots. They are clothes made from cloth which fulfil certain government

Above: The spirit of 'Make Do and Mend'. Vera Lynn in a gingham dress she fashioned from a haul of household dusters. Improvisation was the order of the day. Handbags, for example, were scarce, as they did not come under the Utility scheme – so women mostly made their own from material or crotcheted string. Even the Queen confirmed that she had 'an old hat turned inside out, remade, and it looked like new'. *Left:* Utility bedroom furniture – simple, well-designed and inexpensive.

refinements. . . . If Mayfair hasn't the skill to cut a good dress from three or four yards of material with five or six buttons, it must learn – or go under.' Eventually Utility clothing accounted for about four-fifths of all production.

From July 1940 the supply of timber for domestic use was cut off, and only small quantities had been released to meet the needs of bombed-out families. By 1942 the shortage of new furniture was acute, and the only items available were were badly made and expensive. In August the government prohibited the manufacture of all but twenty-two items of furniture, each with a prescribed timber content. For each of these, two qualities and three designs were specified. Utility furniture's austere lines and matt finish were much sneered at in postwar years, but they made an aesthetic virtue out of necessity and were a small triumph of good design. It also enabled priority groups like young newly-weds to acquire basic furnishings for their home, a task which had previously been all but impossible. Eventually the utility concept was extended to cover a wide range of civilian materials from crockery, linoleum, sheets, blankets and mattresses to pencils, domestic electrical appliances, sports gear and even jewellery. Mrs J. Mikkelsen was married in June 1943 and recalled, 'My wedding ring was a utility one and made of nine carat gold and cost 30s 9d. It was possible to get twenty-two carat gold rings on the black market at £10 each, but my ring has worn well and has never been off my finger.'

As the Board of Trade sternly informed the retail trade:

> IN WARTIME, production must be for war and not for peace. Here are examples of the changeover from peacetime products to wartime necessities:
>
> CORSETS become Parachutes and Chinstraps
> LACE CURTAINS become Sand-fly Netting
> CARPETS become Webbing Equipment
> TOILET PREPARATIONS become Anti-Gas Ointments
> GOLF BALLS become Gas Masks
> MATTRESSES become Life Jackets
> SAUCEPANS become Steel Helmets
> COMBS become Eyeshields
>
> ISSUED BY THE BOARD OF TRADE
>
> You may wish to cut this out and display it to your customers

One doubts that this rather surreal catalogue was much comfort to civilians hunting forlornly for nonexistent supplies of alarm clocks or razor blades. Shortages had turned even the simplest shopping expedition into a consumer's obstacle course. On 27 January 1944 a note of exasperation creeps into Mrs Milburn's diary:

> A few months ago one asked for a toothbrush over a chemist's counter as a matter of course. Lately one has not been able to buy them at all. In fact, most things are 'If we'd got the ham we'd have some ham and eggs – if we'd only got the eggs'. Apples are not seen in the shops at the moment at all, cake shops display bread and rolls, and when the cakes are coming in there is usually a long queue outside. The cake shop in the village has buns and rock cakes day in, day out, and not too many of them. The second window displays bird seed, pickles and even toilet paper in discreet rolls! Sweet shops also display goods unheard of in their trade, for since they can only sell the ration they must, I suppose, deal in other things to keep their shops going.

A patient queue forms for scarce eggs. The queuing habit was so ingrained that it became almost automatic. In Hull in the autumn of 1941 a Mass-Observer found a long queue of about 70 people outside a shop. A young bystander told him, 'I don't suppose they know what they're queuing for. It's hysteria with some people – whenever they see a queue they just join on the end. I expect they end up with two bunches of roses and a stick of rhubarb'.

Soap had been rationed to 16 oz a month since February 1942. Beer and tobacco, although unrationed, were often in short supply. The beer was watered down, as barley was diverted from the breweries to the bakeries. This prompted many a mordant taproom jest: Barmaid (handing Yorkshireman a pint of beer): 'It looks like rain.' Yorkshireman: 'Aye, I thought it wasn't beer.'

Shortages could sometimes have the most melancholy results, as Derek Lambert recalled:

Pets found little comfort in the shortages. At the outbreak of war we had two white mice, a tortoise, a goldfish and a budgerigar.

Bran and oats for the mice soon ran out and for a while they existed on a diet of bread, sawdust and newspaper; then the larger of the two found the answer to rationing and began to eat the smaller. . . . The diet ended one day in 1942 when the small mouse, tired of being eaten, lay down and died. Shortly afterwards the cannibal followed him.

The tortoise left us – a casualty of war – at about the same time . . . One day he strayed into the garden next door, hid beneath some leaves, and had his head chopped off by a spade digging for victory.

There was also a grave and inexplicable shortage of ants' eggs. From inside his bowl Charlie the goldfish made pop-eyed pleas for more food and sent up bubbled distress signals. I found white eggs on ant hills but Charlie ignored them. He ate fish food sold in packets from necessity but was plainly wasting away. He lasted, with fishy resilience, longer than the other pets; then one day he leapt from the bowl and disappeared down the kitchen sink and was never seen again.

'Make do and mend' became the phrase most closely associated with the British wartime drive for self-sufficiency. The shortage of shoe leather led to a vogue for wooden clogs. Women were encouraged to make their own wartime jewellery from beer-bottle tops, corks and cup hooks. In the absence of stockings, many women painted their legs with a commercially produced lotion, which had an alarming tendency to change colour in the light of day. Hard-pressed cosmetic manufacturers supplied small packets of unmixed ingredients for their customers to make up themselves. Women improvised: they used bicarbonate of soda, dusted under the arms, as an anti-perspirant; a mixture of olive oil and chopped beeswax as a skin softener; burnt cork was transformed into eyelash mascara and Reckitt's Blue was applied to lighten grey hair. They prolonged the life of their remaining silk stockings by rinsing them through with methylated spirits and storing them in an air-tight jar. With the shops bare of all but expensive secondhand toys, the WVS stepped in to organize Christmas toy exchanges where 'you could expect to meet four rocking horses, six forts, two tricycles, a doll's house and a brand-new sewing machine, not to mention china tea services, jigsaw puzzles, a whole army of soft toys and dolls and thirty mechanical toys.'

As there were no new tablecloths to be had, the staff of the Granada restaurants made up replacements from a combination of dust sheets and bed linen. Sometimes individuals took the concept of self-sufficiency a little too far. The rationing of crockery led to a plague of petty pilfering, and during one twelve-month period the Granada's chain of restaurants lost about 20,000 pieces. In the home, scarce cleaning materials were supplemented by crushed egg-shells used as a scouring compound for dishcloths made out of old silk stockings cut into inch-wide strips and crocheted into squares. Woodwork was cleaned with tea dregs; old mackintoshes were cut up to provide a bib for baby; the soles of children's shoes were varnished to make them last longer.

In addition to urging the public to 'Dig for Victory', the government launched a campaign to utilize all possible salvage materials. The patriotic housewife was requested to place her salvage in four separate containers: one for tins and other metal, somewhat optimistically earmarked for aircraft and tanks; one for boiled bones, to be turned into glue, again for aircraft, or glycerine for explosives; one for kitchen waste for the feeding of pigs; and one for paper, allegedly for cases for rifles and shells, but more realistically for recycling.

Children were willing helpers in the salvage drive and were officially encouraged by the 'Superintendent Salvage' advertisements which urged mothers to 'make the children responsible for the Salvage Collections. They'll enjoy doing a worthwhile job and they'll probably help you to keep on the mark yourself. The youngsters make good helpers – especially if you appeal to their imagination.' The ensuing dialogue between the short-trousered Superintendent Salvage and his equally small lieutenant, Detective Inspector Waste, makes these tiny toilers of the salvage pile sound like a couple of Men from the Ministry, an effect heightened by the Detective Inspector's bowler hat, which fetchingly complements her pinafore dress:

SUPERINTENDENT: Now, Inspector, let's have your report.
INSPECTOR: Well, sir, everything's mostly according to plan. I have my men in every house and a sergeant acting directly under each grown-up Salvage Steward.
SUPERINTENDENT: Good. How's the Bone Hunt progressing?

"of course there's no harm in your knowing!"

INSPECTOR: Things are moving. My house constables check up on every joint that comes to the house and personally superintend plate clearance after each meal. They are also present at each emptying of the stock pot and take account of all bones given to the dog. These are all reclaimed and put into the Bone Tin. Every other day the house constable takes the tinful to the street collector's post and adds it to the bone collection. . . .

SUPERINTENDENT: Have you tracked down the case of pig-swill poisoning yet?

INSPECTOR: Yes, sir! At No. 4 Home Drive one constable was not alert enough in seeing that *no* coffee grounds and rhubarb tops went into the bucket with vegetable trimmings and plate scrapings. He knows the seriousness of this slackness and won't offend again.

SUPERINTENDENT: Well, carry on, Inspector, and don't forget that the Case of the Elusive Rubber must be tackled next. Not an old hot water bottle, a rubber boot, a worn-out rubber ring, or an old bicycle tyre must escape.

INSPECTOR: Very good, sir. The squad is on the job!

Queen Mary was reputedly a dedicated collector of salvage. In 1943 the writer Godfrey Winn informed the public: 'Queen Mary never uses a new envelope and on the course of her drives to visit camps and aerodromes and factories, wherever she sees salvage lying around un-claimed – bones, bottles, scrap iron – Her Majesty stops the car, has it picked up, and taken home in triumph to the village dump.'

Magazines and newspapers ran regular salvage competitions, award-ing prizes of National Savings certificates for the readers who came up with the best hints. The winners of *Good Housekeeping*'s December 1942 competition were:

Mrs I. Mallabourn, 17 Clareville Road, Darlington: Make a firelighter by shaving one end of a thick piece of wood to make a sort of 'brush'.

Mrs H. H. Butler, 9 Homefield Road, Bromley: Make reversible hessian bag with recipient's name and address on linen label stitched to one side and sender's on similar label on inside, so that laundry may be sent to and fro to members of the forces, etc.

Miss Mary Taylor, 8 Cairnside, E. Herrington, Sunderland: Have week's inter-family competition, with different types of salvage – e.g. books, papers, souvenirs, cardboard – to be saved each day, and points awarded for biggest total. Biggest total of daily points wins prize.

Even blitzed buildings yielded up their quota of salvaged materials. Rubble was used to build runways for the RAF and the USAAF forces stationed in Britain, or as ballast on ships sailing to America where, the story went, it was then used to pave the streets of New York.

Throughout the war Ernest Bevin, the Minister of Labour, devoted as much time to explaining how important it was to dig for coal as other Ministers explained that it was to dig for victory. However, labour shortages and the government's reluctance to nationalize the coal indus-try led to a sharp fall in coal production. In 1943 Bevin took the extreme step of directing a proportion of the young men called up for National Service into the mines. The 'Bevin Boys' were chosen by a ballot of their registration numbers. Those with the unlucky numbers went into the mining industry, although only about 15,000 of those drafted by this unpopular measure served at the coal-face.

Coal rationing, a political hot potato throughout the war, was never introduced, although upper limits were placed on domestic consump-tion. Reliance was placed on 'voluntary rationing' by the public, who were subjected to an intense barrage of exhortations to play their role in

"The price of petrol has been increased by one penny."—Official.

Left: A famous cartoon by the *Daily Mirror*'s Philip Zec, published in March 1942. It enraged the government, which took it to mean that seamen were risking their lives for profiteers at home, and the *Mirror* was briefly threatened with suppression before the row blew over. *Opposite and below:* Some celebrated propaganda messages of the Home Front.

the front line of 'The Battle for Fuel'. 'Fuel Watcher', in the advertisements issued by the Ministry of Power and Fuel, reminded the housewife that the careful use of cinders to light fires in every household would save 750,000 tons of coal a year, '*Remember* that 750,000 tons of coal are used in producing the steel for making 10 battleships.' Another 'Fuel Watcher' advertisement asked, 'Is *your* home helping to build a destroyer?', reminding the reader that '5 lb of coal saved in one day by 1,500,000 homes will provide enough fuel to build a destroyer. Note: 5 lb of coal are used in 2 hours by a gas fire or electric oven.'

Householders were urged to mix coal dust, clay and water to make a 'briquette' which gave out a fitful heat. They saved water by never using more than 5 inches of water in the bath and doing the day's washing-up in one go.

The very nature of a successful black economy defies any attempt to estimate its size. But almost everyone 'knew a man' who could put them in the way of scarce consumer goods if the need arose. There was a flourishing black market in petrol and clothing coupons, and by 1944 the black market value of one clothing book was about £5. Unscrupulous farmers and smallholders exploited the loopholes in food distribution. The slaughtering of animals was supposed to be conducted under rigorous control but, not entirely surprisingly, the 'accident rate' among farm animals soared during the war. Usually there was the shrugged excuse, 'The poor brute broke its leg, so we had to put it out of its misery.'

A number of sharp operators made a quick profit by selling worthless 'substitutes' for commodities now rare or in greater demand. A mixture of flour, salt and baby powder was sold as 'milk substitute' at five shillings a pound. Others peddled cut-rate cosmetics, concocting face powder from chalk dust and cheap scent. Sometimes these 'substitutes' could be lethal; one black market brand of lipstick was found to contain a high admixture of lead.

IS YOUR JOURNEY REALLY NECESSARY?

RAILWAY EXECUTIVE COMMITTEE

Above: Saving became a national obsession during the war. Savings drives included War Weapons Weeks in 1941, Warship Weeks in 1941–42, Wings for Victory Weeks in 1943 and Salute the Soldiers Weeks in 1944. By 1943 the average citizen was saving up to a quarter of his disposable income, not least because there were so few consumer goods on which to spend it. *Left:* Children in a paper drive. At least 100 tons of paper were needed to plan and build a battleship. Six old books provided enough material for one mortar shell carrier. *Opposite, right:* Familiar figures in the war on waste. *Opposite, bottom:* A salvage drive in Belfast. Rags were often difficult to collect – 'We're wearing 'em' was often the working-class housewife's reply.

The king pins of the black market were shadowy figures, most of whom managed to evade the clutches of the law. In films they were invariably portrayed as oily, overdressed types with a veneer of sinister charm. One night a Land Girl, Shirley Joseph, encountered three such men, who gave her a lift in their gleaming limousine.

They all had black hair, smoothed to perfection like the smiling gentlemen in the hair cream advertisements. But they were not gentlemen and they looked as though they never smiled. . . . They spoke in a sort of harsh whisper. 'Here, we've come all the way from Birkenhead and haven't done no business.' 'One thing, petrol's no object.' 'Did you fix that deal for the thousand tyres?'

At the mention of tyres I pricked up my ears. I knew my father had badly wanted some new tyres for a long time.

'What, can you get tyres?' I asked impulsively.

For a moment there was silence. I think they had forgotten my existence.

'Tyres? As many as you want – at the right price,' one answered, laughing without smiling.

7

LET THE PEOPLE SING

If Goebbels wants to see the effects of German raids on British morale, he ought to be in a theatre while an air-raid alarm is on. A big audience simply revelled in a free after-the-show concert by Max Miller, Vera Lynn, Doris Hare and Tommy Trinder the other night. And they chipped in £15 for a Spitfire.

Manchester Sunday Chronicle, September 1940

Vera Lynn, the Forces' Sweetheart, has seldom had a more appreciative audience than she did today when she sang her songs in a Nottingham hospital ward in which were men wounded in the Tunisian campaign.

Nottingham Evening News, July 1943

An Appreciation from a Middle-Aged Listener

I do not as a rule care for crooners, and have learned after due trial to avoid listening to them. But when I was told that a woman was to be a heard in 'Sunday Matinée' who had been voted Favourite Crooner No. 1 by general consent of the boys in the forces, one whose name and songs aroused an enthusiasm that was far more than ordinary, I became curious. So I listened to her. She sang – or crooned – very simply and very slowly, popular ballads of the hour: 'Little Steeple Pointing to a Star', then 'The London I Love', and finally the chorus of 'Over the Hill'. From the audience of troops she had a great reception. I think I know why. For as I listened, time slipped back for me twenty-five years, and I became once again one of a similar audience, khaki-clad and lonely at heart at a concert in some YMCA hut, trying to forget for a while the stress of war and waiting. And that young soldier of an earlier generation found himself at one with the receptive, appreciative, grateful mood of the young soldier audience of 1941.

Radio Times, May 1941

In wartime music fills an important niche in national life. In the Second World War it was not used as a wardrum, to beat up martial spirit, but to provide good cheer for the forces, to stimulate workers in the war factories and to hearten people in their homes. And it gave me the opportunity to talk to the nation through song. When I broadcast my radio show 'Sincerely Yours', I was in a BBC studio, but I always tried to imagine that I was at my own fireside, singing not to a huge unseen audience 'out there' but to individuals with me in the same room. It might have been a young man serving in the Western Desert who missed his wife, or a mother anxious about her son in the Far East. The songs I sang for them were simple, sincere and sentimental in the best sense of the word. They reflected the fears, heartaches and hopes of ordinary folk who missed their loved ones and looked forward to a better world after the war was over. I felt these emotions and believed in these things too. All wars are a time to say goodbye, and the sadness of separation affected everyone. What mattered most to me was the personal touch, so important when people were often separated by vast distances. I was a kind of messenger, linking separated people and, through the words of a song, telling one what the other wanted to say.

Vera Lynn in her ENSA uniform, popularly known as 'Basil Dress', after the organisation's director Basil Dean.

Opposite: Vera Lynn visits a hospital
during the making of 'Sincerely
Yours'. Fellow-broadcaster Wilfred
Pickles paid her this tribute: 'When
Vera visited hospitals and then, on
the Forces Programme, told the
fighting men about their new babies,
she was not merely reading a script;
she really saw every child she talked
about – and took flowers to all the
mothers'.

*And it was the sentimental, wistful songs which the boys in the forces
most wanted to hear.*

*Radio played an enormously important role in the war. The BBC's
programmes, from 'The Brains Trust' to 'ITMA', bound the nation
together. I made hundreds of broadcasts, but the ones which still mean
the most to me were the series of 'Sincerely Yours' request programmes
which began in November 1941.*

*In April 1940 I had been voted the British Expeditionary Force's
favourite singer, ahead of Deanna Durbin, Judy Garland and Bing
Crosby. Soon the BBC was receiving requests from servicemen around
the world who wanted me to sing specific songs on the air. I suggested
to the BBC producer John Howard Thomas – who also produced 'The
Brains Trust' – that I present a fifteen-minute show in which I would
sing some of the requests. One night at the Palladium I was called to the
stage-door telephone. John Howard Thomas was on the line. 'About
that programme, Vera. We're going to do it. It won't be fifteen minutes
but half an hour, and I've thought of a good idea for it. We'll do it in
the form of a letter which you'll send to the boys each week. We'll call it
"Sincerely Yours – Vera Lynn".'*

We slipped on to the air with no great fuss. The billing in the Radio
Times *ran: 'To the men of the Forces: a letter in words and music from
Vera Lynn, accompanied by Fred Hartley and his orchestra.' The
programme's success overwhelmed us. After the first show we were
flooded with requests, and they continued to pour in at a rate of over a
thousand a week. To establish an intimate link with individuals in the
audience, I visited hospitals and nursing homes before the show so that
I could tell Gunner Jones or Bombardier Brown that his wife had just
had a baby, that I had talked to her and that mother and child were just
fine. It was like putting their hands together. Soon I was swamped with
messages from mothers, nurses and even doctors, all wanting me to sing
or send a message to the father in the forces.*

*Not everyone approved of 'Sincerely Yours'. Its success spurred some
killjoys – bellicose MPs and retired generals – to claim that the soldiers'
morale was being undermined by 'sentimental slush'. There was even
an 'anti-slush' campaign at the BBC. It didn't last long. My songs
reminded the boys of what they were* really *fighting for, precious
personal things rather than ideologies and theories. It was this shared
experience which brought me close to the seven million listeners who
tuned in to 'Sincerely Yours' on Sunday night and enabled me to tell the
men in the forces: 'Dear boys . . . it used to be very easy to answer your
letters, because what most of you used to say was, "Please send me your
autograph." But since I started my Sunday broadcasts you've written to
me very differently – as though you know me well, and as though I'm
your friend. . . .'*

Within its broad boundaries the British Broadcasting Corporation,
'Auntie BBC', contained many of the cross-currents and contradictions
of wartime Britain. On the one hand, it frequently censored itself, often
indulged in rather stiffly contrived patriotism and occasionally took itself
far too seriously. On the other hand, it kept the nation laughing with
classic radio comedy, stimulated by its serious music and drama, and
informed on every aspect of life on the Home Front, from health ('The
Radio Doctor') to home-making ('The Kitchen Front'). It also brought
the war dramatically into people's homes. Those who heard them will
never forget the live sound of tanks going into action at Alamein; the skirl

of the pipes as the Eighth Army marched into Tripoli; the report from a bomber over Berlin delivered by Wynford Vaughan-Thomas; and Richard Dimbleby's moving broadcast from the liberated concentration camp at Belsen.

Like the nation itself, the BBC got off to a rather shaky start when war was declared. The evacuation of many of the BBC's departments led to a great deal of improvised programming before the broadcasters settled down in their new billets. On the outbreak of war all regional programmes had been closed down and were replaced by a single Home Service programme. In the early months of the war the Home Service embodied the stuffily high-minded approach which had been the hallmark of Lord Reith, the Corporation's first director-general: hourly news bulletins, interspersed with news flashes, some rather pompous moral uplift and swathes of air time devoted to mournful organ music. In January 1940 the BBC saw the light, introduced the lively 'Forces Programme' and embarked on a mission, successfully accomplished, to become the voice of a united people at war.

Wartime radio quickly threw up a wide range of personalities who became national figures. At the very beginning there was Tommy Handley, star of 'It's That Man Again', universally known as 'ITMA', the anarchic comedy show which became a treasured institution. Its producer, Francis Worsley, recalled 'ITMA's' birth:

> On the 19th September 1939, at 9.30 p.m. . . . 'ITMA' had its real First Night. After a two-hour rehearsal – a long time for those early days of war – we took the floor in the Clifton Parish Hall [in Bristol] before a small audience mainly composed of people on the staff. Outside there was the blackout, responsible for many a black eye, for somehow one was continually walking briskly into lamp-posts or parked cars. Wardens were being very strict about even the tiniest glimmer of light, and we had to creep into the various studios round a complicated system of screens and curtains, carrying our gas masks wherever we went. But once inside the building all was gaiety and light, and a sort of party spirit pervaded the atmosphere. For one thing there was no stage, so that the audience and the artists were all together on the same level, and when they were not actually speaking their lines or performing, the cast sat down, often on grand piano or floor, thus giving the whole thing a very informal air. Thus it was on the first night of the show that was destined to make radio history. Tommy's first words . . . set the topical pace at which we have tried to keep the show going ever since: 'Hello, folks! It's *mein Kampf* again! Sorry. I should say, Hello, folks! It's that *man* again! That was a Goebbled version a bit doctored. I usually go all goosey when I can't follow my proper-gander. . . .'

Thereafter every ITMA show invited its listeners to a kind of national party. The format developed by Worsley and his scriptwriter Ted Kavanagh placed the fast-talking Handley at the centre of a cast of zany characters who popped in and out of each show with bewildering speed, each one signing on or off with a special catchphrase: Ali-Oop, the oriental pedlar ('I go – I come back'); the Diver ('Don't forget the diver' and 'I'm going down now, sir'); Mrs Mopp, the Corporation cleaner with a ready line in ripe double-entendre ('Can I do you now, sir'); Claude and Cecil, the diffident broker's men ('After *you*, Claude', 'No, after *you*, Cecil'); and the bibulous old buffer Colonel Chinstrap ('Don't mind if I do').

Kavanagh's non-stop blizzard of catchphrases, topical quips, excruciating one-liners and surreal story lines aimed for a laugh every eleven

seconds. 'ITMA' was a triumph of pure radio, creating a completely
realized madcap world which took on a concrete reality inside every
listener's head. Inevitably, perhaps, the illusion did not survive 'ITMA's'
transfer to the screen in a feature film of 1943. The sight of so many of the
show's famous characters in the flesh was a disappointment, although
Handley was his usual irrepressible self as His Washout, the Mayor of
Foaming-at-the-Mouth, sinking the entire council budget into a blitzed
London theatre. It's hard to resist a comic who can effortlessly get away
with such awful one-liners as 'I kissed my mother-in-law – with a lighted
cigar!'

In any one week 16 million people listened to 'ITMA', and its
catchphrases burrowed their way into the fabric of everyday life. Home
Guard units were instructed to confront suspected enemy parachutists
with a demand for a line from Colonel Chinstrap or Mrs Mopp; a small
boy, trapped under a pile of rubble after an air raid on Bath, piped out to
the rescue squad, 'Can you do me now, sir?'

'ITMA' was pre-eminent in a golden age of radio comedy. But close
behind came 'Big-Hearted' Arthur Askey and Richard 'Stinker' Murdoch
in 'Band Waggon', Robby Vincent, Harry Korris and Cecil Frederick in
'Happidrome', and the Americans Ben Lyon and Bebe Daniels, who had
settled in London and co-starred with Vic Oliver (Winston Churchill's
son-in-law) in 'Hi, Gang!'

The Corporation kept a careful eye on its comedians, and in November
1943 the Variety Department, rattled by the short-lived 'anti-slush'

campaign, issued a set of guidelines which speaks volumes for wartime sensibilities. In addition to the existing ban on 'blue gags' and jokes about illness and deformity, the BBC placed an embargo on the following: the Home Guard, the black market, the police, American soldiers, the ATS, WAAF and WRENS, the bombing of German civilians, officers (although fun at the expense of sergeant-majors and NCOs was permitted) and drink. Entertainers were also instructed to avoid the use of the word 'blimey' and 'other similar expressions'; and to steer clear of 'the Southern expression "Yes, Suh" accent', except in Kentucky minstrel routines.

At nine o'clock every night life in 10 million British homes came to a halt as families gathered round the wireless for the News. The BBC's news bulletins became increasingly important as paper shortages shrank daily newspapers from twenty-four sheets to as few as four. At the same time the Corporation's newsreaders, immaculately attired in evening dress as they read their scripts, acquired a remarkable degree of celebrity. As the announcer Joseph MacLeod explained in his autobiography:

> The fall of France affected our work. Invasion seemed more than likely, at any moment. Instructions would have to be given by announcers under such circumstances that no voice could succeed in issuing false instructions even if the enemy seized a station. Therefore the public must recognize our voices. . . .
>
> We were called together to agree the best formula. One was required which would be neat, accurate and memorable; preferably something new, which would make a hit with the public and be burlesqued on the halls and in the comic papers. This plan was deliberate and succeeded. The formula finally chosen was, 'This is the BBC Home Service. Here is the News and this is —— reading it.' . . .
>
> Yet I never got used to using my own name. It sounded indecent to me. I couldn't forget that I was bursting into a room where two or three people were sitting in chairs talking. Never in private life do I burst into strangers' rooms and say, 'Stop talking. I'm Joseph MacLeod. Listen to me. There's been a great naval victory at Cape Matapan, and Jim's ship has been mentioned.' And yet after some months we were their intimate friends, and many of them had a feeling that we knew all about Jim and his ship.
>
> And after a few more months, one learned to drop the voice in shops when one gave one's name. Otherwise people turned round and stared.

Throughout the war the News was broadcast from London, even at the height of the Blitz. Bruce Belfrage became a national hero when a near miss on Broadcasting House, clearly audible as he spoke, caused only the slightest pause in his delivery. From time to time reading the news had its lighter side. After the war Belfrage recalled an incident during the Blitz.

> Whenever the war news allowed enough time, we used to read out the football results after the six o'clock bulletin on Saturday evenings. I had finished this operation and was groping my way across the road for a breath of fresh air and a glass of beer, when I was pursued by one of the commissionaires with a message that I was urgently required on an important trunk call from Scotland. I hurried back, but at least fifteen minutes must have elapsed from the time the call was put through, and I assumed the matter must be extremely critical if a trunk line could be occupied for so long. Rather anxiously I picked up the receiver.
>
> 'Hullo – this is Belfrage here – who is that?'
>
> 'Never you mind who it is – are you the ignorant bastard who has just read the News?'

'Well, I . . .'

'Do ye no ken that the football team from this city is the Glasgow Seltic?'

'Oh, is it? I always thought C-E-L-T-I-C was pronounced Keltic.'

'Well, all I can say is that if that's all the education you have, you have no business to hold your job down.'

'I am very sorry you feel so upset about it, but I . . .'

'Upset? It's a disgrace – no wonder the country is in a mess – you'll hear more of this, I'm telling you.' And the receiver went back with a crash.

As he was speaking, the nightly ration of bombs had begun to fall.

Immediately after the Nine o'Clock News on 5 June 1940 listeners heard a warm, relaxed Yorkshire voice asking them, 'I wonder how many of you feel as I do about this great battle and evacuation of Dunkirk?' The comfortable voice was that of the writer J. B. Priestley, whose radio 'Postscripts' (subsequently broadcast every Sunday after the Nine o'Clock News) were small masterpieces of homely patriotism, couched in the deceptively casual language of the thoughtful pipe-smoking chap with whom you might strike up a conversation in the pub. While Winston Churchill rallied the nation with stirring images from our past, Priestley concentrated on small-scale but telling aspects of wartime life: a night spent in the country with a Home Guard unit; a drunk bawling 'Rule Britannia' in an air-raid shelter; a confrontation with an overbearing official; a visit to the seaside resort of Margate, melancholy and bereft of its holidaymakers. Priestley's talks were steeped in the naturally gentle temper of the British and their hatred of bombast and bullying: 'Let the Nazis in,' he warned, 'and you will find that the laziest

Vera Lynn in a BBC studio. On the extreme left is the urbane figure of Alvar Lidell, doyen of announcers, who brought news both good and bad to the public in tones of patrician calm.

loudmouth in the workshop has suddenly been given power to kick you up and down the street.'

Priestley's brand of populism quickly attracted criticism that it had a left-wing political slant. On 21 July 1940 he launched an attack on property, which, he felt, should give way to the notion of 'community': 'And I'll give you an instance of how this change should be working. Near where I live is a house with a large garden that's not being used at all because the owner of it has gone to America. Now, according to the property view, this is all right, and we, who haven't gone to America, must fight to protect this absentee owner's property. But on the community view this is all wrong. There are hundreds of working men not far from here who urgently need ground for allotments so that they they can produce a bit more food. Also, we may soon need more houses for billeting. Therefore, I say, that house and garden ought to be used whether the owner, who's gone to America, likes it or not.'

These sentiments struck a chord with Priestley's audience but set alarm bells ringing in the government. His second series of 'Postscripts' was stopped, as he recounts in his autobiography:

> When I was brought back, after much clamour, I added some minutes and more edge to my talks. This time I was taken off the air . . . I received two letters and one was from the Ministry of Information, telling me that the BBC was responsible for the decision to take me off the air, and the other was from the BBC saying that a directive had come from the Ministry of Information to end my broadcasts. While blaming each other, I think that both of them were concealing the essential fact – that the order to shut me up had come from elsewhere.

Perhaps the most improbable radio stars of the war were a philosopher, a zoologist and a retired naval commander. They were respectively Professor Cyril Joad, Julian Huxley and Commander A. B. Campbell, the original members of 'The Brains Trust', which went on the air for the first time on 1 January 1941. Under the suave chairmanship of Donald McCullough, 'The Brains Trust' fielded a stream of questions, sent in by listeners, ranging from abstruse philosophical points to the celebrated 'How does a fly land on the ceiling?' Joad, with his squeaky voice and famous opening phrase, 'Well, it depends on what you mean by . . .', became an overnight celebrity and the butt of many a comedian's patter – so much so that the BBC's Variety Department attempted to ban jokes about 'The Brains Trust'. The bluff Campbell was the perfect foil for Joad, speaking for the man-in-the-street and spicing his answers with many an old seadog's tall tale; in reply to a question about allergies he cited a friend who was so allergic to marmalade that, on eating it, steam rose from the top of his head.

At the peak of its popularity 'The Brains Trust' had a regular audience of 11 million. The BBC ensured that the verbal pyrotechnics of its stars did not get out of hand by limiting each answer to one minute and scrupulously avoiding controversial issues like equal pay for women.

Male and female war workers were spurred on to greater productivity by 'Music While You Work', relayed by loudspeaker across the factory floor. 'Worker's Playtime', which made its debut on 31 May 1941, was broadcast three times a week from a factory canteen during the lunch break. By May 1943 over 250 factories had been visited, 330 programmes transmitted and 270,000 workers entertained. Vera Lynn appeared on the 200th 'Worker's Playtime', which came from a factory in the west of Scotland. Other popular shows were built around particular aspects of the war effort. Among them was 'Ack Ack – Beer Beer', which showcased talent found among the men of Anti-Aircraft, Balloon Barrage and Searchlight units. There was even a soap opera, forerunner of 'Mrs Dale's Diary' and 'The Archers', focusing on the trials and tribulations of a 'front-line family' called the Robinsons.

There was something for everyone on the BBC, whose great river of programming flowed on untroubled by the titanic events of the war. On the night of 7 September, as London's dockland blazed in the first big raid of the Blitz, listeners to the Home Service could hear a concert by the WAAF choir, a show presented by the comedian Cyril Fletcher, a Beethoven concert, a talk on 'Picture Postcard Beauties', the news in Norwegian and Gaelic, the 'Nine o'Clock News' and – as the night's destruction reached its climax in the Surrey Docks – 'Pig Hooo-o-o-ey!', a dramatization of one of P. G. Wodehouse's most famous stories, set in the rural never-never land of Blandings Castle.

The war was the BBC's finest hour. In September 1939 it had 4233 personnel and employed twenty-three transmitters with a total power of 1620 kW to broadcast for fifty hours a day. In 1945 it had a staff of 11,417, and 138 transmitters with a total power of 5250 kW, and was broadcasting for 150 hours a day, many of them in forty-seven foreign languages. For the people of occupied Europe it was the voice of freedom.

The radio voice of the enemy was 'Lord Haw Haw'. This was William Joyce, a former member of the British Union of Fascists, who had offered his services to the Nazis at the beginning of the war. The name 'Lord Haw Haw' was first used in the *Daily Express* in September 1939, but had been applied not to the harsh-voiced Joyce but to the ludicrous upper-class drawl of another renegade broadcaster, Norman Baillie Stewart, a former subaltern in the Seaforth Highlanders. However, it was quickly

The ebullient radio-journalist Wynford Vaughan-Thomas takes his microphone down into a submarine.

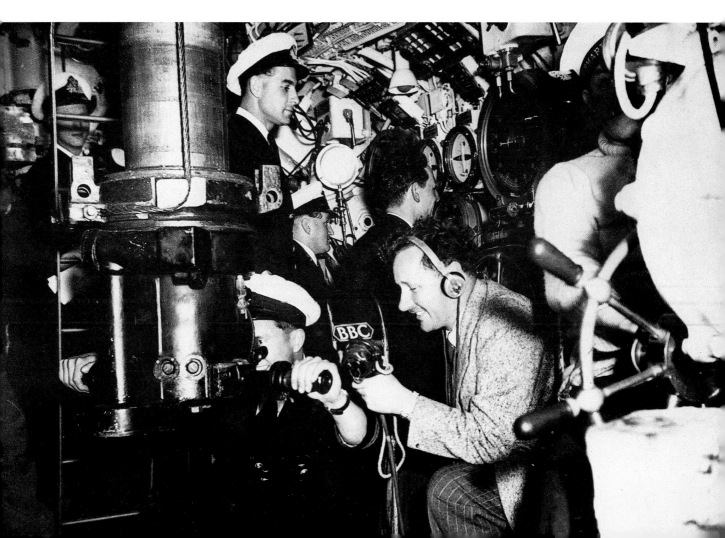

Dame Myra Hess photographed during the series of morale-raising concerts she gave at the National Gallery. One of her recitals is quirkily caught on film by Humphrey Jennings' evocative wartime documentary film, *Listen to Britain* (1942).

appropriated by Joyce, who became the Nazis' chief English-language broadcaster.

Joyce's propaganda was a curious mixture of fact and fiction, not without a weird sense of humour and larded with misfiring colloquialisms inserted on the orders of his masters. On one occasion he announced that a battleship had sunk 'after being hit in the kettles'. He began each broadcast with 'This is Jairmany calling', in a parody of an upper-class accent, and this catchphrase became almost as popular as any dreamt up for 'ITMA' by Ted Kavanagh. In time Lord Haw Haw gained a sinister, if spurious reputation for omniscience, informing his audience of the precise time at which a town hall clock had stopped or where a new factory was being built. More telling, perhaps, were some of the fictional characters he introduced into his broadcasts, among them a Jewish millionaire (Sir Izzy Ungenheimer), a hypocritical clergyman (Bumbly Mannering), and a fatuous diplomat (Sir Jasper Murgatroyd), who occasionally came uncomfortably close to tapping deep-seated wells of British prejudice.

No attempt was made to jam Lord Haw's Haw's broadcasts, and the times and wavelengths could be read in *The Times* alongside those of the BBC's programmes. During the Phoney War Joyce's fulminations exercised a considerable fascination, and in January 1940 a government survey showed that one out of every six British adults, including 30 per cent of *The Times*' readership, was a regular listener. In his own bizarre way Joyce briefly became a radio personality to rank alongside Tommy Handley or Bruce Belfrage; a revue called *Haw Haw!*, described as 'a new laughter show', enjoyed a successful run at the Holborn Empire in the summer of 1940.

136

Joyce's run continued until the very end of the war, when he signed off, roaring drunk, in the ruins of the Third Reich. Not long afterwards he was arrested by the British at Flensburg, in north Germany, and taken to London to be tried for high treason. His only defence was that he was an American citizen (he had been born in New York) and therefore not legally able to perform acts of treason against the British. However, the prosecution stated that for the first nine months of the war he had held a British passport and therefore did owe allegiance to the crown. He was sentenced to death and executed in 1946.

Wartime conditions transformed conventional attitudes towards classical music and theatre, both of which found vast new audiences which had been untapped by the commercial system in the 1930s. In the autumn of 1939 the pianist Dame Myra Hess launched a celebrated series of concerts at the National Gallery which continued throughout the Blitz. The Council for the Encouragement of Music and the Arts (CEMA) was founded in 1939, with the aim of employing out-of-work artists and organizing musical activities for evacuation centres. This evolved into a system of 'music travellers', who criss-crossed the country, playing for communities far from a concert hall. CEMA then expanded into the theatre, providing the funds for a tour of South Wales and County Durham by the evacuated Old Vic, led by Sybil Thorndyke and Lewis Casson. In the autumn of 1942 CEMA established its own theatrical circuit, with fourteen touring companies, and funded initiatives like open-air 'utility' performances of ballet and opera in public parks. Sadler's Wells toured industrial towns with a company of twenty-six and an orchestra of four; the decor for their production of *The Marriage of Figaro* consisted of two chairs and a sofa. By 1943 CEMA was giving over 4500 factory concerts a year. It also sponsored 'Art for the People' exhibitions, which took the work of the best British painters the length and breadth of the nation.

An ENSA mobile recording unit, a small miracle of 1940s streamlining, presented by Gertrude Lawrence, herself a stalwart performer for ENSA during the war years.

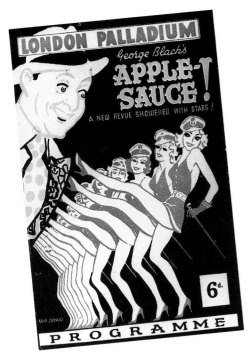

The plain-speaking Ernest Bevin once confided to Basil Dean, the director of ENSA (Entertainments National Service Association), that he considered CEMA 'too 'ighbrow'. In contrast much of ENSA's output ran little risk of this charge, although it had its serious side too.

ENSA was born in August 1939 and was the brainchild of Basil Dean, the theatrical producer and film magnate, who had been a pioneer of troop entertainment in the First World War. Dean, a hard-driving autocrat who made many enemies during the war, was convinced that in the coming conflict servicemen would need, and demand, professional entertainment. His plan was to organize his own army of artistes, covering the whole range of the entertainment business, who would be prepared to go anywhere to entertain the men in the forces.

On the outbreak of war ENSA established its headquarters at the Theatre Royal, Drury Lane, and on 9 September dispatched its very first concert party to entertain troops of the Scots Guards waiting at Pirbright Camp to be sent to France. ENSA had been quick into the field, but the early months of its life were dogged by a combination of muddle and acrimony which clung to it throughout the war. Much of this was due to factors beyond ENSA's control. When war was declared, a 6 p.m. curfew was imposed in the West End, sending London shows and revues to the provinces. When it was lifted, productions flooded back to the capital, and by the turn of the year there were more shows in the West End than there had been twelve months before. Artistes were reluctant to abandon good wages in the West End for the ENSA rate of £10 a week or £4 in the chorus.

Inevitably ENSA was overwhelmed by applications from enthusiastic amateurs and unsuccessful professionals who relished the modest security of an ENSA contract. At this stage in the war many of the stars were making their own private arrangements to entertain the troops, and the quality of ENSA's shows was, to put it mildly, extremely variable. However, Dean's policy was to meet any demand rather than provide a more limited service, and in this he succeeded. By the end of November 1939 ENSA had 700 artistes on its books and had given 1492 shows, which had been seen by 600,000 people.

Stan Tracy, later one of Britain's leading jazz musicians, recalled the early ENSA days: 'The people I worked with were not much as performers, nobody of any quality. We had two old birds, Ninah and Norah; my God, they must have been sixty! They did a juggling act which was pathetic. There were a couple of soubrettes, one of whom was a big, jolly, plump-buttocked girl who fell on her arse nearly every night – she was terrible – a blind siffleuse, an impressionist and conjurors who had the most ghastly magic tricks, one in front of the magic set you buy for your kid.' It was ENSA shows like these – immensely game but irredeemably fifth-rate – which earned Dean's organization the nickname 'Every Night Something Awful'.

ENSA struggled to overcome its teething problems. Concert parties dispatched to remote locations often became hopelessly lost, as all signposts had been removed to confuse German paratroops. When they did arrive, they provided a much-needed morale boost for the men on lonely Ack-Ack and balloon sites. ENSA also had the distinction of taking the first film show to the island of Barra in the Hebrides. When the Gaumont newsreel began, with the figure of the old-time watchman ringing the bell, the islanders 'stampeded, bowled over the operator, trod on his projector and vowed never again to enter the "haunted hut"'.

ENSA also crossed the Channel to entertain the BEF in France, where

Above: The programme for *Applesauce!*, in which Vera Lynn co-starred with Max Miller, 'The Cheeky Chappie'. Its opening, at the Holborn Empire, coincided with the start of the Battle of Britain. The Holborn Empire was badly damaged during the Blitz, and the show eventually found a new home, at the Palladium, in March 1941, while the bombs were still falling. *Opposite:* 'We Never Closed!' Windmill girls prepare for a performance. For a brief period during the Blitz the Windmill theatre, with its staples of low comedy and bare flesh, was the only theatre open in London. As a result its showgirls became something more than mere sex symbols.

Gracie Fields sang to huge audiences. In the freezing winter of 1939–40 the troops were kept laughing by George Formby and Will Hay and sang along with the bands of Joe Loss and Billy Cotton. By the beginning of May 1940 there were over 200 ENSA artistes playing to the BEF. Their shows were rudely interrupted by the German Blitzkrieg, and many ENSA performers accompanied the British troops evacuated from Dunkirk, while others escaped from French ports farther to the west. All of them were back in London by mid-June. The BEF had been forced to abandon all its heavy equipment in France, but the only items left behind in the ENSA evacuation were a few property baskets.

Back in a Britain under siege ENSA faced new demands. In addition to entertaining Londoners during the Blitz there was now pressure to send performers to the Middle East. A new recruiting drive was launched, and in May 1942 ENSA became the Department of National Service, a branch of the Civil Service, with Dean as its director. In spite of the new nomenclature, everybody still called it ENSA.

Dean was now modifying his approach to the range of entertainment provided by ENSA. As the comedian Charlie Chester observed, at the beginning of the war the accent had been on 'tits and tinsel'. But with the call-up of older age groups and the mixing of the classes in the services, the ENSA programme was expanded to include more of the 'highbrow'

The tireless George Formby entertaining Tube shelterers during the Blitz. Formby performed prodigies for ENSA, and led the first concert party to arrive in Normandy after D-Day. His film comedies were popular in the early years of the war, but by 1945 his brand of broad Northern humour had fallen out of favour with cinema audiences.

entertainment of which Ernest Bevin was so suspicious. ENSA's Good
Music section promoted concerts by artists of the calibre of violin
virtuoso Yehudi Menuhin, the pianists Solomon and Moura Lympany
and Sir Adrian Boult and the BBC Symphony Orchestra, which gave the
first ENSA symphony concert for the Army in May 1943. Boult was
delighted to learn that he had broken the previous box-office record (set
by Gracie Fields) by 1s 9d – dramatic proof that in wartime classical
music was not merely the province of the artistically minded minority but
could have a mass appeal.

ENSA performed wonders overseas, often in the most gruelling and
hazardous conditions, entertaining troops from North Africa to Burma.
In the spring of 1944 Vera Lynn toured the Arakan Front in Burma, and
she still remembers the slap of the huge jungle insects dive-bombing her
accompanist's piano keys as they homed in on the lights of her improvised stage.

ENSA followed the Allies into Normandy on 24 July 1944, when six
parties, led by the indefatigable George Formby and his ever-present wife
Beryl, landed in France. ENSA accompanied the drive through the Low
Countries, establishing its headquarters in Brussels, where it remained
until the end of the war. It was fitting that ENSA was in at the death. With
Montgomery's troops at Luneburg Heath, where the German forces in
the West surrendered, was a three-handed concert party. That night they
gave a show, lit by the headlights of six jeeps. Little had changed since the
early days of 1939 – the pianist's music was blown away by the wind. But
on this occasion nobody seemed to mind.

Vera Lynn made three wartime films – *We'll Meet Again* (1942), from which the song sheet is taken, *Rhythm Serenade* (1943, *right*) and *One Exciting Night* (1944, *above*). In *We'll Meet Again* she virtually played herself, a dancer who become a radio singing star. In *Rhythm Serenade* she was 'the girl next door', with Ben Warris (left) and Jimmy Jewel (right) providing comic relief as her brothers. *One Exciting Night* gave a more dramatic role, mixed up with art thieves. In all three films there are lots of songs.

ENSA was disbanded in 1947. At its peak in the war it was mounting some 500 shows a week at home and abroad. In Britain every factory on an approved list of 1000 was visited by one or two ENSA parties every week performing in the canteen during lunch breaks. By the end of 1944 ENSA was employing nearly 4000 artistes, and during the war years approximately four-fifths of the British entertainment profession had appeared under its banner, playing to a combined audience of millions. Many of the stars of the future began their careers in an ENSA show. Essentially a civilian organization in a military world, it attracted its fair share of criticism, from the supposedly 'blue' jokes of comics like Tommy Trinder to its erratic appearances in remote theatres of war. But the relief, laughter and occasional enlightenment it brought to civilians and servicemen during the war remain its true monument.

The outbreak of war had temporarily threatened to close down the British film industry, then in the throes of one of its recurring periods of crisis. For two weeks in September 1939 the cinemas were shut, a measure prompted by fears of mass death at the height of an air raid, and a number of them were set aside for the storage of thousands of cardboard coffins. Simultaneously a large amount of studio space was requisitioned for use in the 'shadow factory' scheme and for storage. In 1939 there had been twenty-two studios operating sixty-five sound stages; by 1942 the numbers had fallen to nine studios with thirty-five sound stages. At Pinewood the sound stages assumed the unglamorous role of warehouses for sugar and flour. A 'hush hush' unit of the Royal Mint was also established at Pinewood, prompting the jibe that for the first time the studio was making money. The call-up and wartime shortages were also to take their toll. By the winter of 1940 Ealing Studios had lost about a quarter of its relatively small workforce of 200. Ultimately, about two-thirds of the industry's pre-1939 technicians were called up. Sets were built from salvage wood, packing materials, hessian and plaster. Obsolete equipment was nursed along by expert servicing. Coupon allocations for costumes had to be wheedled from the Board of Trade. One evocative photograph of the period shows an Ealing Studios music sound track being rehearsed by musicians in overcoats and mufflers. All this was in keeping with the 'make do and mend' philosophy which lasted throughout the war and into the peace that followed.

The film-going habit was deeply ingrained in the British public, and when the cinemas reopened the queues were soon winding round the block for Clark Gable and Vivien Leigh in *Gone with the Wind*. The Blitz failed to dull the national appetite for films. One Londoner recalled, 'I shall never forget the night the Café Anglais was hit. All hell was let loose that night. The corner block was down. A huge fire was blazing. Twenty or thirty fire engines were tearing round the square. And there was still a long queue of people waiting to go in to see *Gone with the Wind*.'

By the end of the Blitz in May 1941 audiences had climbed back to peacetime levels. The wartime historian of the Granada chain wrote:

> They queued patiently in the dark when aircraft were droning overhead; they sat through films while the building was rocked by near misses, and glass and plaster showered into the auditorium, while the film jumped on the screen or the spotlight bounced from the stage to the ceiling; they put out incendiaries in the stalls and went on with the show; they came with rugs and hot-water bottles when the heating failed, and when part of the roof was blown off and the rain came in, they moved into a part of the theatre where it was dry; when their homes were hit, they came back the next morning with the bomb dust still in their hair, and when the cinema

was hit* they climbed over the rubble in the street to ask when it would reopen. In none of sixty bomb incidents in cinemas which I have investigated was there any suggestion of panic – not even when a bomb burst in an auditorium during a performance. So far from subscribing to pre-war official view of a cinema as a potential deathtrap, patrons came to regard it as a refuge, a strength and an escape. Audiences actually felt safer in cinemas and were more sharply affected by the film on the screen than by the conditions that reigned outside.

Some diehards were almost impossible to shift. On 24 August 1944, at the height of the V-1 campaign, the Granada in West Ham had a close shave.

It was 6.30 p.m. and there were 600 people in the theatre watching a somewhat appropriately named film, *Block Busters*, with Tod Slaughter in *Crimes in the Dark House* as second feature.

Up in the operating box Second Operator Flo Gristwood was on the machine and a girl trainee-operator was keeping a lookout. She had as close a view as anyone ever had of a flying bomb coming down. It just missed the theatre flagpole and landed on The Greyhound, a pub barely 100 yards away.

The girl trainee was thrown from the ladder and Flo Gristwood and a junior rewind girl were blown across the box, together with glass and debris, as a considerable part of the roof disappeared. Flo Gristwood stopped the machines and went to the assistance of the other girls. All members of the theatre staff were bruised and shocked by the blast (all Manager Keep's teeth were loosened and had to be extracted), but the audience escaped injury.

In fact, Chief Operator Chapman, walking through the theatre some time after the explosion, was surprised to see several youths still sitting in their seats. They asked somewhat indignantly if he was not going to finish the show – and that with rain pouring in and neither roof nor doors on the theatre.

Over 80 per cent of the films seen by wartime audiences came from Hollywood, a land of impossible glamour in austerity Britain. The production of homegrown features fell to an average of about sixty a year, but the drop in quantity was more than offset by an increase in quality. However, this was not immediately apparent, as the British film industry went through its own Phoney War before finding its feet and a fresh sense of purpose.

The first film of the war was Alexander Korda's *The Lion Has Wings*, released in November 1939, a strained combination of documentary and drama which featured Ralph Richardson and Merle Oberon as a 'typical' British couple and a risible sequence in which a massed German air fleet turns for home the moment it sights the balloon barrage over London. With some honourable exceptions, the films of the first eighteen months of the war bowed to the conventions of the 1930s, on to which wartime plots were sometimes painfully grafted: in between bouts of furious ukelele-bashing George Formby uncovered nests of Nazi spies; and stern-jawed officer types stepped straight out of the drawing room on to the battlefield, where it was the other ranks' job to provide comic relief before dying conveniently off screen while their superiors hogged the heroics.

---

* Of Britain's 4000 cinemas, 160 were totally destroyed during the war, 60 of them in London.

Above: Nasty Nazis – Raymond Lovell points an accusing finger at Will Hay, who is masquerading as a German master spy in the wartime comedy *The Goose Steps Out* (1942). A very young Peter Ustinov is the bespectacled stormtrooper on the extreme left. Seated in the centre are, left to right, Barry Morse, Charles Hawtrey and Peter Croft. *Left:* Factory foreman Eric Porter and 'mobile woman' Patricia Roc in Launder and Gilliat's moving evocation of wartime sacrifice and solidarity, *Millions Like Us* (1943).

Above: Picturegoer salutes Margaret Lockwood and the darkly handsome James Mason, stars of *The Wicked Lady* (1945). *Left:* John Mills, as Able Seaman 'Shorty' Blake, and Kay Walsh in Noel Coward's *In Which We Serve* (1942). *Below, left:* Roger Livesey as Colonel Blimp, sweating it out in the steam room of the Royal Bather's Club in Powell and Pressburger's *The Life and Death of Colonel Blimp* (1943). *Below, right:* George Formby unmasking a nest of Nazi spies in *Spare a Copper* (1941).

The mould was finally broken in 1942 by Noël Coward's *In Which We Serve*, which followed the career of a destroyer, HMS *Torrin*, from her commissioning, through action in the North Sea and at Dunkirk, to her sinking during the evacuation of Crete. Coward wrote, produced and co-directed the film (the last with David Lean) and starred as *Torrin*'s captain, a character he modelled closely on his friend Louis Mountbatten, whose own command, HMS *Kelly*, had suffered the fate celebrated on celluloid by *Torrin*. *In Which We Serve* broke new ground by devoting equal time to officers and men. The film remains very conscious of class distinctions but nevertheless presents *Torrin* as a community bound together by common danger and working together for a common end, like the nation of which it is a microcosm. Coward's Captain Kinross now seems somewhat stiff and studied, although his quiet farewell to the crew as they are paid off is an object lesson on how to end a film successfully on a dying fall. Among the ratings John Mills was outstanding as able Seaman 'Shorty' Blake, and Richard Attenborough made a memorable debut as a stoker who loses his nerve under fire. *In Which We Serve* created a big impression in America, where it won a New York Critics Award and a special Academy Award.

The influence of the realist school of film-making, fostered in the 1930s at the GPO Film Unit by John Grierson, found an outlet in a stream of superb documentary and propaganda films, among them *Target for Tonight* (1941), *Listen to Britain* (1942), *Fires Were Started* (1943) and *Western Approaches* (1944). The impact of the documentary approach on the waging of the 'People's War' can be seen in feature films like Ealing's *San Demetrio, London* (1943), based on a real-life incident in which the crew of a crippled tanker nursed her back to port; Launder and Gilliat's *Millions Like Us* (1943), a moving drama set among 'mobile women' in a war factory; and Carol Reed's *The Way Ahead* (1945), an

Cartoonist Acanthus sends Mrs Miniver and Vera Lynn into the attack in North Africa.

"You, Daisy Perkins, will lead the attack, supported by Mrs. Miniver and Vera Lynn."

army version of *In Which We Serve*, which followed a platoon of infantry recruits from training to their baptism of fire in the Western Desert. These films focused on the lives of ordinary soldiers and civilians with a degree of restraint and realism which contrasted sharply with glossy Hollywood tributes to the British like *Mrs Miniver* (1942) and *The White Cliffs of Dover* (1944).

Resolutely swimming against the realist tide were the director-screenwriter team of Michael Powell and Emeric Pressburger whose richly romantic fantasy of 'Englishness', *The Life and Death of Colonel Blimp* (1943), was perhaps the finest film of the war. Very loosely based on the exploits of Low's reactionary cartoon hero, the film enraged Churchill – something of a Blimp himself – who felt that *The Life and Death of Colonel Blimp* would hold the Army up to ridicule. He tried, and failed, to have the film suppressed, his defeat representing a minor triumph of the democracy the Allies were fighting to defend.

The mid-war years of 1942 and 1943 saw public interest in war subjects rise to a peak and then fall away; ironically, by the time the British had real victories to celebrate the popularity of war films had diminished. In January 1944 a Bristol woman wrote to her local newspaper: 'I've just seen the Bette Davis film *Now Voyager* and what enjoyment and what relief – no war.'

This mood was tapped with immense success by Gainsborough Studios in *The Man in Grey* (1943), the first in a series of bravura costume melodramas which were treated with undisguised disdain by the critics and undisguised enthusiasm by a public yearning for undiluted escapism. *The Man in Grey* made a star of the brooding James Mason, giving full rein to his powerful blend of arrogant good looks and cultivated misogyny. Mason played the sadistic Marquis of Rohan, whipping his mistress Margaret Lockwood to death, to the evident satisfaction of the readers of *Picturegoer* magazine, who voted him Actor of the Year. Women adored him as the vicious Lord Manderstoke in *Fanny by Gaslight* (1944), tormenting Phyllis Calvert and duelling to the death with flashily handsome Stewart Granger; and as concert pianist Ann Todd's lame guardian in *The Seventh Veil* (1945), bringing his cane crashing down on her hands in a frenzy of impotent rage.

The British film industry approached the end of the war in a mood of great optimism. Annual cinema admissions had climbed to the 160 million mark. Laurence Olivier's spectacular *Henry V* – filmed in Eire – had scored an immense prestige success in the United States and won Olivier a special Academy Award. Films like *The Seventh Veil* were making inroads into the American market. Our leading directors – Michael Powell, Anthony Asquith, Carol Reed, David Lean – were at the height of their powers. The stimulus of war had propelled our cinema into a brief golden age which lasted until 1949, the year in which Ealing's *Passport to Pimlico* poignantly evoked the rapidly dissolving bonds of wartime solidarity.

8

WOMEN AT WAR

Vera Lynn with the two Land Girls
who worked on her Sussex farm
during the war.

She's the girl that makes the thing
that drills the hole that holds the spring
that drives the rod that turns the knob
that works the thingumebob

When the Second World War began in September 1939 the British
government was already forearmed with the knowledge of the contribution women had made to the war effort in the First World War. In the
earlier conflict the decision to extend employment opportunities to
women had been taken with the greatest reluctance. In the interwar
years, however, women had played an increasingly prominent role in
clerical and light industrial work – as early as 1929, 25 per cent of those
employed in the non-industrial Civil Service were women – and this had
paved the way for the challenges they were to face on the Home Front in
the Second World War.

Ironically, the early mobilization of women echoed a feature of
1914–18, reintroducing female labour to an overwhelmingly male preserve, Britain's farms. The Women's Land Army, which had been an
innovation of the earlier war, was re-formed in June 1939 under the
vigorous leadership of Stella, Marchioness of Reading. By the outbreak
of war the WLA numbered 1000 volunteers; by the harvest of 1941 there
were 20,000. The numbers eventually peaked at about 80,000, of whom
one-third were from London or other big cities.

The word 'Army' was something of a misnomer. The Land Girls were
issued with a uniform – green jersey, brown breeches, brown felt slouch
hat and khaki overcoat, often eccentrically modified to suit personal taste
– but were subject to no discipline other than dismissal (which usually
meant redirection into the auxiliary services or war industry). They had
to work where they were sent, but were denied the use of forces' canteens
in their snatched hours of leisure. They were entitled to only seven days'
leave a year, compared with twenty-eight days in the military, and
frequently had to pay their fare home. Many girls, uprooted from
familiar surroundings, suffered the pangs of homesickness in bleak
hostels.

Newspapers and films tended to present an idealized view of the Land
Girl. The film critic C. A. Lejeune, writing about Bernard Miles's rural
comedy *Tawny Pipet* (1944), gently mocked 'the slim, selected figure of a
land girl, leading a gee-gee, with the future mirrored in her brave, steady
eyes'. The 'Land Army Song', with its bracing equation of farming with
fitness, reinforced the image:

Back to the Land, we must all lend a hand.
To the farms and the fields we must go.

There's a job to be done,
Though we can't fire a gun
We can still do our bit with the hoe. . . .

Back to the land, with its clay and its sand
Its granite and gravel and grit.
You grow barley and wheat
And potatoes to eat
To make sure that the nation keeps fit. . . .

We will tell you once more
You can help win the war
If you come with us – back to the land

Land Girls as the Ministry of Information liked to see them, bursting with vitality and bathed in sunshine. The reality of life on the farm was sometimes very different.

The reality was often different. After the war Rachel Knappett wrote about her experiences as a Land Girl in south Lancashire:

Of all the jobs that we do, I think that knocking muck is the most gruelling. The neat little piles that the carters have left down the furrows have to be knocked with forks, so that the muck lies level in the bottom of the furrow. The knocker walks crabwise on the ridge and bends nearly double to hit the muck with his fork in the furrow. Sometimes the muck is light, dusty stuff, mostly sawdust, and one wallop with the fork scnds it flying to the next pile in a most encouraging way. This sort of muck, beloved by the knockers and cursed by the boss because its value as manure is negligible, is very rare. It is usually heavy, sodden and rich, and has to be shaken and persuaded and bullied into going in the right direction.

I often wonder if I shall ever forget the searing ache that knocking muck produces in the small of the back, and all the nagging muscles that it

151

discovers in the wrists and shoulders. I know I shall never forget the day when Marjorie [a fellow Land Girl] was first introduced to the business.

It was a very warm day in April. We had started knocking at seven o'clock in the morning and had been at it steadily until four in the afternoon. For the last few hours Marjorie had been finding it heavy going. Her chin was jutting out and her teeth were clenched with determination. Her face was streaked with earth and sweat. Suddenly she stuck her fork into the drill and slowly, with agonized grimace, she straightened her back. She bent weary, dejected eyes upon me, and said dramatically:

'Rachie, I think I'm going to die!'

Remembering my own struggles of two years before, I tried to find a few comforting words of sympathy. Marjorie cut short all such banalities by adding:

'Not that I mind much if I do.'

Knocking muck is not a job that is over and done with in half an hour; it goes on for weeks and weeks.

In spite of the back-breaking toil of muck knocking, or the long-drawn-out agony of lifting sprouts in the mud and gloom of a November afternoon, the wastage rate in the WLA was lower than that in industry, the attraction of 'life on the land' surviving experience of it.

Some 25 per cent of Land Girls were employed on milking and general farm duties. Others worked in threshing gangs, a dusty, dirty business which took its toll on delicate complexions. Some became specialists. About 1000 Land Girls were employed as rat-catchers; two young women in Lincolnshire accounted for 12,000 of the vermin in a single year. Six thousand entered the WLA Timber Corps, felling trees, working in sawmills or selecting trees for felling, the last a lonely job which took them over hundreds of miles of remote countryside, where they were occasionally suspected of being spies.

Farmworkers eyed newly arrived Land Girls with equal suspicion. Acceptance, when it came, was all the more heartwarming for being completely unaffected. One day soon after her arrival Rachel Knappett collided with one of the labourers.

'Cum art road, yer gaupin' bugger,' said Alec [in south Lancashire this was a term of friendly abuse]. The men turned round in horror. Then, seeing that I was laughing and not flat on the floor in a swoon, they joyously received the word back into their vocabularies, their tongues were loosened and the sun shone more brightly. From that moment, for better or worse, I began to belong to Bath Farm. Instead of being addressed in a stiff and formal manner, I became 'Owd yaller 'ead', 'Owd Knappoo', 'the bloody wench', 'Sparrer', 'the poot', 'gaupie', 'blondie', or 'oo' (she).

Lady Reading, who had revived the WLA, was also the founder in 1938 of the Women's Voluntary Service (WVS), an organization formed with government approval and with the original intention of drawing women into the ARP. The membership was essentially middle class, mirrored in the uniform for which the WVS volunteers had to pay – a grey-green tweed suit, beetroot-red jumper and felt hat reminiscent of the type worn by the heroines of Angela Brazil stories. The ranks of the WVS were filled with the kind of well-meaning well-to-do women who presided over church fêtes, and in its early days was the object of some ridicule. But when war came it transcended its plummy-voiced image to channel the energies of thousands of women into the urgent task of plugging the myriad gaps in the Home Front. As a Mass-Observation report of September 1940 put it, the WVS 'acts as a kind of maid-of-all-work to the established authorities'.

Members of the WVS serving with the Queen's Messenger's Convoys, which stayed on alert to rush hot meals to any badly bombed town. By 1941 there were over a million WVS volunteers, with only 200 paid staff. The WVS did sterling work throughout the war. During the Battle of Britain one member of the WVS in Yorkshire reported to HQ: 'General Position satisfactory. One German parachutist captured by me yesterday' – she had disarmed him with a pitchfork.

This was at the beginning of the Blitz, in which the WVS played a vital role. The Mass-Observation report continues:

> The Stepney Branch of the WVS has only been formed within the past few months, but in the present emergency it has been doing excellent auxiliary work, providing helpers for the municipal authorities for evacuating the homeless and other tasks, assisting with transport, and operating mobile canteens for ARP, AFS [Auxiliary Fire Service] and other war workers. For example, when the investigator visited the people's palace on Saturday afternoon, September 21, he was told that the WVS had taken over from the municipal officials who had gone home at 1 p.m., and had evacuated 200 people.

In the Blitz the WVS seemed to be everywhere. In the last six months of 1940 it received and distributed £1.5 million worth of clothing, mostly from America and the Commonwealth. Its national network of dumps held the bulk of Britain's gift clothing, ready for emergency issue. The WVS set up a 'Housewives' Service', which enabled women to play a part without even leaving the street in which they lived, providing ARP workers with hot cups of tea and bomb victims with warm blankets, and keeping a careful census of residents for the use of the air-raid wardens. The Ministry of Health invited the WVS to help with the evacuation and care of unaccompanied or orphaned children. On the day after the Coventry raid of 14–15 November 1940 WVS mobile canteens drove into the centre of the city to serve hot stew in the smouldering, shattered streets. Later its members staffed the Queen's Messenger's Convoys, comprising eighteen fleets each of twelve vehicles, which remained on constant alert to rush hot meals to any badly bombed town; the convoys performed particularly valuable work in Liverpool and Plymouth. In 1943, in conditions of the utmost secrecy, WVS volunteers provided meals for the engineers building the huge artificial Mulberry harbours which were to be towed across the Channel to Normandy in June 1944. More prosaic was the WVS's 'Rural Pie Scheme', established in 1942, in which the 'ladies in green' victualled farm labourers working in the fields; at its peak the scheme was distributing over a million pies and snacks a week in 5000 villages.

Women had worked as bus and tram conductresses in the First World War, and in 1940 they became 'clippies' again. Older passengers eyed the trousers they wore with some distaste, but traditional notions of what women should wear quickly gave way to wartime practicality. A writer visiting an industrial region in 1942 after a long absence noted: 'Before the war, slacks and shorts were worn by girls – mostly of the leisure class – for holidays and sports wear. Now they are wearing trousers to do their work. Milk girls, window cleaners, drivers, railway workers, bus conductors – all are dressed for the job. If the war goes on much longer it may be a sign of eccentricity for a young woman to wear a skirt.'

The conscription of women was introduced in December 1941, an unprecedented measure which went far beyond anything contemplated by Hitler or Stalin. The National Service Act (No. 2) applied to unmarried women between twenty and thirty; nineteen-year-olds were brought in in 1942, and in 1943 the upward age limit was raised to fifty-one,

Women were quick to fill the jobs vacated by men serving in the forces – from clipping tickets on the buses to driving milk floats.

PIMLICO CAMPAIGN FOR WOMEN FIRE GUARDS
MAY 11 to 16 1942
WE MUST HAVE ENOUGH FIRE GUARDS
IT IS UP TO ALL WOMEN WHO CAN TO HELP

Vera does her bit, appealing for women to join the Fire Guard, formed in mid-1941 as an adjunct to the warden's service. Its first big test came with the Baedeker raids in the spring of 1942. At this period women between the ages of 20 and 45 had been made liable for fire-watching, and training had been made compulsory for the first time.

principally to release younger women for work in aircraft factories. Married women not living apart from their husbands were wholly exempt, as were women with children under the age of fourteen. The conscripts were given a choice between serving in the auxiliary services – the WRNS (Women's Royal Naval Service), the ATS (Auxiliary Territorial Service) and the WAAF (Women's Auxiliary Air Force) – civil defence or industry. Those who chose the auxiliary services would not be called upon to handle a lethal weapon unless they signified their willingness to do so in writing. About 25 per cent of all 'mobile' women – some 460,000 – chose the women's auxiliary services. A social survey conducted in 1942 revealed that 97 per cent of women agreed 'emphatically' that they should undertake war work.

By mid-1943 the proportion of Britain's women who were serving in the forces, munitions works and essential industries was about double that in 1918. The number of married women and widows employed on war work had risen from the 1939 level of 1.25 million to 3 million. Nine out of ten single women between the ages of twenty and forty were in the forces or industry. It was virtually impossible for a woman under forty to avoid war work unless she had heavy family responsibilities or was looking after a war worker billeted on her.

In some factories there was initial resistance to the arrival of women war workers. There was no shortage of 'little woman' mockery, leg-pulling requests for 'rubber drills' and furtive leering. Mark Benney described the male workers' reaction to the first woman to arrive in the installation section of an aircraft factory in 1941: 'We looked at her, nine of us, for days as though we had never seen a woman before. We watched the dainty way she picked up a file, with red-enamelled fingertip extended as though she were holding a cup of tea. We watched the way she brushed the filings off her overalls after every few strokes, the awkward way she opened and closed her vise, her concern for the cleanliness of her hands, her delicate, unhandy way with a hammer. . . . Behind her back we had great fun mimicking her; to her face we treated her with an almost desperate punctilio.'

Right: Women at work in a wartime shipyard, previously an all-male preserve. *Below:* Filling shells in an ordnance factory. In factory or shipyard, the home-made turban soon became a universally adopted safety measure to protect hair at work. Later, the disappearance of hairpins led to the adoption of the short 'Liberty Cut', promoted by *Woman's Own* magazine in 1942, which was more practical and hygienic.

Left: Women apply more traditional skills to a flock of barrage balloons. *Above:* Women became expert welders, particularly adept at intricate work requiring finesse and attention to detail.

Opposite: Rescue workers at
Farringdon Market in 1945 after a
V-2 attack. A quarter of all Civil
Defence workers were women.
These included members of the
Auxiliary Fire Service (both full- and
part-time) and the air raid
ambulance service. The majority of
the ambulance drivers were
women, often working in conditions
of great danger. Initially they were
entitled only to lower rates of
injury compensation than men.

For many young women the first days in the noise and bustle of a big factory came as a shock. In peacetime Rosemary Moonen had been a hairdresser and 'a somewhat genteel, reserved type of girl':

To be plunged abruptly into a world of coarse, ill-bred men and women, where language was foul and bluer than the bluest sky, was an experience so harsh and unreal that, had God not endowed me with a true, strong sense of humour, I fear I should have floundered and stayed wretchedly unhappy for the rest of the war years.

The factory was vast, and I was told to report for the night shift. Although quite a few of the girls had been recruited from other walks of life, like me, most of them were real rough-tough die-hards, heads swathed in turbans, sporting curlers beneath, cigarette dangling, loud-voiced and hard-faced. They eyed all newcomers suspiciously, and were most unfriendly until one's face . . . eventually blurred into the pattern. I was sent with group of die-hards to report to a certain foreman. He surveyed us all, grimly gave each one a job to do, with the exception of yours truly. No doubt I looked nervous and scared. He ignored me, and as he turned to walk away I said, 'What shall I do?' He turned toward me, sneered, 'Oh, yes! We've forgotten sunshine here! What shall you do? – Here! Take this!' indicating a broom, 'And sod off!' . . . The day foreman was much nicer and more polite, and as time went on I found my niche. As they discovered I could work a certain machine and get good results, I was transferred to another department. The girls by now accepted me and I was no longer treated with suspicion. Many of the men with whom I worked tried to date me, but as most of them were married, their wives and children evacuated, I declined all offers and invitations. Even the foul language began to flow over my head, and the coarse dirty jokes which prevail in factory life I ignored. More new girls arrived on war work. Models, secretaries, housewives, shop assistants and even a solicitor's wife and a doctor's daughter. I made many friends, and there was a solid cameraderie between us all, and we shared moments of sadness and moments of sorrow.

Wartime films, notably Launder and Gilliat's *Millions Like Us* (1943), painted a sentimentalized picture of women's industrial war work, with much emphasis on ENSA concerts in the canteen and hops at the local army base. Nevertheless, they accurately reflected the social mix of young women drafted into war work. A young schoolteacher who spent her summer holidays working in a factory producing anti-tank mines wrote in her diary: 'Chief topic of conversation was the Dizzy Blonde. She arrived last Monday and has caused quite a sensation, partly by her appearance – wonderful peroxide curls, exquisite make-up, etc. – but much more by her conversation. Has told everyone that she has never worked before as she has an allowance and is going to frame the first pound note she gets. Another tale runs that she lost a wallet with £100 in it, but "just didn't bother"; she's saving up for a fur coat, a really good one; "I had 5 but I've given 3 away". Mrs Barratt's comment, "Now we know what *she* did before the war."'

In some light-engineering plants women constituted up to 80 per cent of the workforce. They proved expert welders and equal to many heavy physical tasks, which were no problem for older women used to humping small children and loaded shopping baskets around.

To a large extent this represented an acceleration of peacetime trends rather than a feminist revolution. It did little to shake the foundations of male prejudice. In the factories women were paid considerably less than men and attracted the hostility of working men, who felt that a woman's place was in the home and that admission of women to traditionally

male-held jobs would lead to unemployment after the war. In 1942 a North Country factory manager wrote in a report: 'The girl has so taken to machinery that she'd like to become an apprentice and go right through the works. This of course is not possible on account of Union agreements. There's a feeling among the men at the moment that women must be in the factory solely because of the war but really women's place is in the home. . . .'

Even in the services most women were confined to their old roles, in the kitchen or at the typewriter. There were exceptions: the women employed in RAF control rooms; those who operated predictors in anti-aircraft batteries; and the mechanics and drivers in the ATS. Entrenched attitudes died hard, and often direct appeals to women's femininity were made as part of the industrial war effort. The public relations officer to the Ministry of Supply declared that 'cosmetics are as essential to a woman as a reasonable supply of tobacco to a man,' and the Royal Ordnance Factory issued a booklet to its female workers, *ROF Beauty Hints: Look to Your Looks*. A welfare officer at a munitions factory was of the opinion that '£1000 of cosmetics, distributed among my girls, will please them more than £100 in cash.' One feels that he hadn't asked 'his girls' about this. Married women who were struggling to get by on their wages and the 25s a week allowance they received while their soldier husbands were away might have given him a very dusty answer.

For those who remained in the home housework was dignified as a contribution to the war effort. The government's 'model housewife' was keen to do 'even better than usual. I shop with special care. I waste nothing. I save paper, tin, bones. . . . I try to keep myself and my house trim and cheerful. I take special pains with the cooking because I know this keeps the men's spirits up. I send the children to bed early and I don't stay up listening for sirens. I remind myself in this way, though I may not be winning medals, I am certainly helping to win the war.'

And, if she followed the advice of *Vogue*, she remained dedicated to the task of 'maintaining the good spirits of the family man. . . . And what do hers depend on? Well, largely on her looks. The business of looking beautiful is definitely a duty. When you look at your best, you feel self-confident and your confidence transmits itself to those around you.'

These sentiments were echoed by Susan Drake in the pages of *Good Housekeeping*:

> . . . at the risk of being called frivolous or superficial, I'm sticking to my opinion that a woman's job of keeping herself attractive is as important now as ever it was. This is as true of older women as younger folk. . . . I'm not suggesting for one second that it isn't both right and vitally necessary to be economical, but lean periods are the times of all times to be as attractive as possible. Moreover, by keeping up the good work in a small way, but with regularity, we spend less in the long run. The habit of Letting Yourself Go has a way of leading to the inevitable moment when you can't stand yourself as you are for another second, and by that time repairs and a general overhaul run into a lot of time as well as money.
>
> War work and war-time conditions keep us frightfully busy. But remember this: Interesting women are busy anyway, war or no war, and these are the women who realize that some of that busy time is wisely spent in keeping themselves as others like them to look.

The virtues of the middle-class housewife were hymned in this popular wartime morale-boosting song:

'Good Morning, my sweet'
I say to my Brenda
She cares for my home
And I'd die to defend her
She mends my old vests
And she takes out the pup
And she sees to the kids
Now that Nanny's called up
She checks up the laundry
And flatters the cook
Then she goes to the library
And gets me a book
Her housekeeping money
Is twelve bob in credit
That ration book form is OK
For she's read it
She's vamped our old grocer
And brought back a tin
Of sardines and some cheese
and a bottle of gin
She's a pearl of a wife
No man could have better
So I kiss her good morning
And then I forget her

But the wartime lot of the average woman was more accurately and more poignantly evoked by Louis MacNeice in 'Swing-Song':

I'm only a wartime working girl.
The machine shop makes me deaf,
I have no prospects after the war
And my young man is in the RAF
  K for Kittie calling P for Prue . . .
  Bomb Doors Open . . .
  Over to You . . .

Night after night as he passes by
I wonder what he's gone to bomb
And I fancy in the jabber of the
  mad machines
That I heard him on the intercom.
  K for Kittie calling P for Prue. . . .
  Bomb Doors Open . . .
  Over to You. . . .

Opposite: One in every six air raid wardens was a woman. This prompted Peak Frean to angle a series of advertisements in a way which speaks volumes for the role of many women in wartime as both war workers and home maker.

Throughout the war the Royal
Family shared the experiences of
their subjects. *Above:* Princess
Elizabeth, serving as a subaltern in
the ATS, is wreathed in smiles as
work is completed on an engine in
the spring of 1945. *Right:* George VI
and Queen Elizabeth inspect bomb
damage at a Baker Street cinema
during the blitz. After Buckingham
Palace was bombed the Queen
commented, 'I'm glad that we've
been bombed. It makes me feel that
I can look the East End in the face'.

Left: The King and Queen meet wounded servicemen at Preston. *Below:* The moment of victory. The Royal Family and Churchill acknowledge the cheers of the crowd from the balcony of Buckingham Palace on VE-Day. Later Princess Elizabeth and Princess Margaret mingled with the crowds in the streets near the Palace. Princess Margaret recalled, 'Everyone was knocking off each other's hats and we knocked off some too.' Later that night the King struck a tender and slightly melancholy note in his diary when writing of his daughers: 'Poor things, they have never had any fun yet'.

Right: The King and Queen inspect women of the Land Army in Cambridgeshire in June 1942.

9

INVASIONS

Over, there, over there,
Send the word, send the word over there,
The Yanks are coming, the Yanks are coming,
Drum, drum, drumming everywhere.

Hitler never launched Operation Sealion, the invasion of England, but this did not save communities throughout Britain from invasions of another kind. Between 1939 and 1945 there were some 60 million changes of address among a population of 38 million. Wartime upheavals left few untouched, producing a constant ebb and flow of internal migrations. By June 1943 the Blitz, evacuation and call-up had reduced London's population to 76 per cent of its prewar level and Southampton's to 67 per cent; in contrast, the population of Reading had increased by nearly 15 per cent.

At the same time small rural towns like Chelmsford, Malvern and Chippenham became centres of war industry, the sometimes reluctant hosts to workers directed to the 'shadow factories' established with government backing in the late 1930s to cope with the increased armaments demands of the coming war. Mass-Observation reported on a small town near Chippenham, in Wiltshire, which had billeted soldiers, relocated civil servants and was now the site of a new war factory employing a thousand workers. The report noted that its previously sleepy streets now resembled 'a London railway terminus, with its endless comings and goings of strangers from all parts of the country; with its atmosphere of irritable bustle, impersonal pushing and hurrying.' The factory workers had appeared 'without warning . . . to eat up the already scarce food supplies; to buy up all the favourite brands of soap and patent medicines; to consume all the fish in the fish-and-chip shops . . . to cram the local cinema at weekends.'

Overcrowding and inadequate accommodation often combined to produce tensions similar to those experienced in Malvern, which in 1942 received the thousand staff of the Telecommunications Research Establishment, which played a vital role in the development and exploitation of radar. Its superintendent wrote: 'The average citizen of Malvern did not want us. . . . Potential billetors fell ill with alarming regularity and the number of destitute aunts who were being given permanent homes in a few days' time passed all bounds of reason. Some gave shelter on the understanding that billetees were in by ten o'clock at night while others gave it on the understanding that they stayed out, somewhere, until the same hour.'

Many a relocated civil servant resented leaving London for the provinces, although there were clear benefits to be gained from leaving the bombs behind for country air. But they brought with them the habits of a wider world, which enriched the cultural and artistic lives of the small communities in which they were billeted. The demand they created for

Strange travellers on the Tube. Some of the National Gallery's paintings are removed to safety at the beginning of the war.

164

Vera Lynn serves Canadian troops with a friendly cuppa.

social services and entertainment of a wider kind than had been usual in the provinces outlasted the war.

In the late 1930s refugees, both Jewish and non-Jewish, had fled to Britain from Nazi persecution. By September 1939 some 68,000 German, Austrian and Czech refugees had found asylum in Britain. When war broke out they were classified in three groups. The 'A' class comprised openly hostile aliens (and our own disaffected citizens), and most of them were interned within a few days. The 'B' class contained 'borderline' cases, including those who had recently arrived in Britain. The majority found themselves in the 'C' class – German or Austrian nationals who had lived in Britain for at least six years and political or racial refugees from continental Europe.

During the Phoney War the 'C' class aliens were free to go about their business. In May 1940, with the threat of invasion looming, official and public attitudes underwent a sharp change. On 12 May the Home Secretary, Sir John Anderson, ordered the internment of about 2000 'enemy aliens' living in sensitive coastal areas. A few days later, in conditions of secrecy, the round-up of the 'B' class aliens began. For some who had suffered at the hands of the Gestapo it was too much; they committed suicide. There were numerous examples of unfeeling bureaucratic cruelty. A seventeen-year-old Jewish boy who had been found a place at Winchester by a barrister was suddenly arrested because the school was in 'a prohibited area'. Before his ward could find the lad another school, he was deported to Canada.

Alien internees begin their journey to the Isle of Man.

The national press did not cover itself with glory during this sorry episode, urging the government to 'intern the lot'. For a fleeting moment the mood of the British public turned ugly. When Italy declared war on France on 10 June there were attacks on Italian-owned restaurants and ice-cream parlours. Internment was now extended to cover 4000 Italians who had lived in Britain for less than twenty years. And by the end of July the net had taken in the majority of the 'C' class aliens.

The plan was to move the internees to the Isle of Man before deporting them to the British Dominions. In the meantime they were housed in transit camps, often in harrowing conditions. At Wharf Mills in Lancashire the internees were detained in a derelict, rat-infested cotton factory. Blankets and medical facilities were virtually nonexistent, the food inedible, radios, newspapers and books banned, and harsh censorship applied to letters. Husbands and wives were separated and families split up with no knowledge of the whereabouts of sick and elderly relatives. An inmate of an internment camp at Huyton wrote: 'The two men who succeeded in committing suicide had already been in Hitler's concentration camps. Against these they held out, but this camp has broken their spirit.' There was a terrible incident at the beginning of July when the *Arandora Star*, bound for Canada with 1500 German and Italian internees aboard, was torpedoed and sunk off the west coast of Ireland. A number of those who drowned had been prominent opponents of Hitler.

Finally tolerance and decency prevailed. At the end of August the issue of internment was debated in the House of Commons, and Sir John Anderson came under heavy fire from all sides. A Conservative MP, Major Cazalet, declared, 'Frankly, I shall not feel happy, either as an Englishman or as a supporter of this government, until this bespattered page of our history has been cleaned up and rewritten.'

The release of internees began almost immediately, and by 1943 the overwhelming majority of aliens (including many Belgian, Dutch and Polish refugees) were helping the war effort, some of them in scientific positions of the greatest importance. Without them the atom bomb would not have been developed. For those who remained temporarily in the Isle of Man, conditions improved and the place became more like a holiday camp than a place of internment.

From September 1939 to the summer of 1940 successive waves of refugees washed our shores. First, Poles who fled their country after Hitler's four-week Blitzkrieg; then, eight months later, Danes and Norwegians; and finally, following the collapse in the West, Dutch, Belgians and the French. The Canadian Charles Ritchie noted in his diary: 'Refugees are beginning to arrive from the Continent – tough-looking Norwegian seamen with shocks of coarse blond hair, dressed in blue serge suits, lunching at Garland's Hotel – Dutch peasant girls in native costume like coloured photographs in the *Geographical Magazine* – walking down Cockspur Street carrying their worldly possessions tied up in bundles. A group of Dutch soldiers in the street in German-looking uniforms gives one a turn. (Shall we see German soldiers in London streets?)'

The presence of Commonwealth and Allied troops added an exotic flavour to the everyday British scene. On Christmas Day 1940 Charles Ritchie was at a country railway station where he saw: 'bold-eyed Canadians – with a slouch and a swagger, New Zealanders with overcoats hanging untidily, Australians, often with girls, and English soldiers going back to London saying goodbye to plain, loyal wives wearing spectacles and sometimes carrying babies.'

As successful with the girls as the Australians were the Poles, many of whom were stationed in Scotland. They quickly gained a reputation for dash and elaborate gallantry towards the fairer sex, something not always appreciated by British husbands and boyfriends. One popular joke of the time was that a memorial should be erected to all the Scottish women who fell for the Poles. The number of entries under Z in the present-day Glasgow telephone directory testifies to their continuing presence in Britain.

With Gallic flair the French in London brought a touch of boulevard life to Soho. Their unofficial centre was the legendary York Minster pub, run by the extravagantly moustachioed Monsieur Berlemont. Writing about the French colony in *Good Housekeeping*, Peter Stafford noted:

Here the company usually includes bearded *matelots* exchanging badinage with waiters from the Savoy, and lovely French dressmakers transplanted from the Rue de la Paix to Grosvenor Street. The atmosphere in the French pubs in Soho is a strange and not unattractive mixture of Britain and France; the talk in many languages and the jokes universal, though broad. Recently the French have been complaining, half-jocularly, that their pubs have become too popular among writers, actors and stockbrokers, delighted to find some new local colour in Soho, whose one-time glory has been diminished by the war and the blackout.

A sad huddle of refugees from Belgium and Holland, surrounded by their meagre belongings, wait to board a bus in London on 18 May, 1940.

Film star James Mason (left) presides over a pile of food parcels from the United States.

And then there were the Americans. The Yanks, as they were universally known, had made their presence felt long before the United States entered the war after the Japanese attack on Pearl Harbor on 7 December 1941. During the Blitz the Savoy Hotel had virtually been taken over by American newsmen. Among them was the brave, resourceful and articulate Ed Murrow, whose nightly broadcasts brought the war starkly home to his fellow-countrymen. The American poet Archibald MacLeish was moved to write to Murrow: 'You burned the city of London in our homes and we felt the flames that burned it. You laid the dead of London at our doors and we knew that the dead were our dead – were all men's dead – were mankind's dead – and ours.'

In more flamboyant mould was Quentin Reynolds, epitome of a breed now long since vanished, the hard-drinking foreign correspondent wise-cracking his way straight from the pages of Damon Runyon. Reynolds covered most of the Blitz from a bar stool in the Savoy Grill. His rasping voice can still be heard, providing the commentary to Humphrey Jennings' documentary *London Can Take It* (1940), which was given widespread screening in America.

The Eagle Club in London's Charing Cross Road was the magnet for the gallant American airmen who fought as volunteers in Fighter Command during the Battle of Britain and flew in the Ferry Service. They were few in number but behind them lay the almost limitless economic might of the United States. In a broadcast to the United States in February 1941, Winston Churchill appealed to his audience to 'give us the tools and we will finish the job'. A month later the Lend-Lease Act gave President Roosevelt the power to lease or provide goods and services to any nation whose defence he considered vital to the security of the United States. This was almost, but not quite, a declaration of war on Germany. Huge amounts of machine tools and foodstuffs were shipped across the Atlantic, and in May fifty American oil tankers were transferred to Britain. Ultimately there was a price to be paid for Lend-Lease. Britain had to sacrifice her gold reserves and overseas investments and restrict her exports. American businesses moved into markets which hitherto had been exclusively British. But as the economist John Maynard Keynes observed, 'We threw good housekeeping to the winds. But we saved ourselves and helped to save the world.'

The first American troops landed in Belfast on 26 January 1942. Each GI had been given a booklet, *A Short Guide to Britain*, which painted an incisive sketch of the British character, in war and peace and underlined the cultural differences between the Americans and their transatlantic cousins:

> In their major ways of life the British and American people are very much alike. . . . But each country has minor national characteristics which differ. . . . For instance: the British are often more reserved in their conduct than we. On a small crowded island where 45 million people live, each man learns to guard his privacy carefully – and is equally careful not to invade another man's privacy.
>
> So if Britons sit in trains and buses without striking up conversation with you, it doesn't mean that they are being haughty and unfriendly. Probably they are paying more attention to you than you think. But they don't speak to you because they don't want to appear intrusive or rude.
>
> Another difference. The British have phrases and colloquialisms of their own that may sound funny to you. You can make just as many boners in their eyes. It isn't a good idea, for instance, to say 'bloody' in mixed company in Britain – it's one of their worst swear words. To say: 'I look like

a bum' is offensive to their ears, for to the British this means that you look like your own backside; it isn't important – just a tip if you're trying to shine in polite society. . . .

Britain may look a little shop-worn and grimy to you. The British people are anxious to have you know that you are not seeing their country at its best. The houses haven't been painted because factories are not making paint – they're making planes. The famous English gardens and parks are either unkempt because there are no men to take care of them or because they are being used to grow vegetables. British taxicabs look antique because Britain makes tanks for herself and Russia and hasn't the time to make new cars. British trains are cold because power is needed for industry not for heating. The trains are unwashed and grimy because men and women are needed for more important work than car-washing. The British are anxious for you to know that in normal times Britain looks much prettier, cleaner, neater. . . .

The British of all classes are enthusiastic about sports. . . . Cricket will strike you as slow compared with American baseball but it isn't easy to play well. . . . The big professional matches are often nothing but a private contest between the bowler (who corresponds to our pitcher) and the batsman (batter) and you have to know the fine points of the game to understand what is going on. . . .

Some Important Do's and Don'ts

Be friendly but don't intrude anywhere it seems you are not wanted.

If you are invited to eat with a family don't eat too much. Otherwise you may eat up their weekly rations. . . .

Don't try to tell the British that America won the last war or make wisecracks about the war debts or British defeats in this war.

Never criticize the King or Queen. . . .

The Americans burst upon the British with all the brash vigour of a Technicolour Hollywood extravaganza. With their bounce, swagger, superbly tailored uniforms and casual generosity, they seemed the living embodiments of a million dreams nurtured in the back row of the Odeon or the Gaumont. The GIs were cocooned in their bases, scaled-down replicas of America, where they enjoyed the high standards of affluence and attributes of their civilization, including their own newspapers, radio and films. They emerged to shower bemused local populations with artless demonstrations of their material abundance. Their PXs poured forth fat packets of Lucky Strike and Camel cigarettes (at 3d for twenty), nylon stockings, chewing gum, Hershey bars, tidal waves of ice cream, canned tomatoes and peanut butter and soap of pre-war quality. The only commodity they seemed to lack was liquor, for which the GIs made up by threatening to drink local pubs dry. There was often a shortage of glasses for the warm beer the Americans found so mystifying, and small boys did a roaring trade, swapping jamjars for Hershey bars.

There was no limit to the ingenuity of small boys when it came to gathering in the American harvest. J. H. Leakey, a schoolmaster who had been evacuated with Dulwich College preparatory school to a village in Wales, wrote: 'Whilst American convoys were going through the village we noticed that one of the tanks frequently checked for a short time by the front door, and then started off again. It was not until I chanced to be outside that day that I realized what was happening. One of the more ingenious boys, whose bedroom window was on a level with the tank turrets as they passed, had found it very convenient to hang out a pole with the notice, "Any gum, chum?" and a kind of fishing net attached, and, again until I discovered it, was reaping a very rich reward from our gallant allies.'

Left: Glenn Miller and his Orchestra, 'somewhere in England'. Miller was lost in a light 'plane over the Channel in December 1944. *Right:* A little bit of America in Piccadilly – the pinball machines in Rainbow Corner, the US servicemen's club in the heart of London. The pinball machines had been collected from the piers and arcades of closed-down seaside resorts. *Below:* A swirl of jitterbuggers at Rainbow Corner. *Below, right:* The rural calm of Dorset is undisturbed by the exotic new arrivals. *Below, far right:* A platoon of black GIs gives a demonstration of 'Jazz Marching'.

Brenda Devereux recalled the arrival of the Americans in Bournemouth:

They swaggered, they boasted, and they threw their money about, bringing a shot in the arm to business, such as it was, and an enormous lift to the female population.

'Come on, babe. How about you and me steppin' out, huh? Gee, you look cute, babe, no kiddin'. . . .'

How those gorgeous GIs could shoot a line, and how we loved it. Not only that, but they were equipped up to the eyebrows with scented soap, cigarettes, food, sweets and dozens of other things we had not seen for years. They were so generous to everybody, it was just like Christmas. . . .

Almost every night found me dancing on an excellent but crowded floor to one of America's top-line orchestras. Coca-Cola flowed as champagne, there was plenty to eat, it was like finding an oasis after a long trek through a burning desert.

American boys were the master of the jitterbug craze, we English girls took to it like ducks to water. No more quick-quick-slow for us. This was really living.

But it was not just their dancing which took us by storm, but their charm and manners. I found myself being waited on hand and foot, with every little whim gratified, they even put on one's dancing shoes on bended knee. I returned home each evening with enough soap, cigarettes and candy to stock a shop. . . .'

Anticipating the moral fall-out of this irresistible affluence, the WVS strove mightily to protect the GIs from the attentions of so-called 'good-time girls', setting up over 200 British Welcome Clubs to supplement the American Red Cross Clubs and encouraging private hospitality. By 1945 a combination of hospitality and PX nylons had produced about 80,000 'GI brides' who sailed with their husbands to the United States at the end of the war.

One aspect of American life imported by the US services – the colour bar – puzzled and disturbed many Britons. There was separate accommodation for white and coloured troops, who were encouraged to patronize different pubs and cinemas in their off-duty hours. The great majority of British people were opposed to this kind of segregation, but the government, reluctant to make waves with its ally, adopted a more ambivalent attitude. Its instructions as to the advice which should be given to British service personnel included this item: '. . . for a white woman to go about in the company of a Negro American is likely to lead to controversy and ill-feeling. It may also be misunderstood by the Negro troops themselves.' Popular attitudes were more forthright. When a vicar's wife in the Somerset village of Worle told her husband's parishioners that if a local woman kept a shop and a coloured soldier entered, she must serve him but 'must do it as quickly as possible and indicate that she does not desire him to come there again,' the *Sunday Pictorial* commented that all black Americans should be assured that 'there is no colour bar in this country' and that 'the vast majority of people here have nothing but repugnance for the narrow-minded, uninformed prejudices expressed by the vicar's wife.'

By the spring of 1944 there were 1,421,000 Allied, Dominion and Colonial troops squeezed into Britain, the majority of them American. Central London reverberated with their presence, attracting crowds of sightseers, among them Mrs Robert Henrey:

I used to join in the procession on Sunday afternoon towards five o'clock, when Shepherd Market was half asleep. . . . Traffic in Piccadilly was so

'Over-paid, over-sexed and over here' was the reaction of some Britons to their American guests. Others found the attentions of a friendly Yank irresistible.

GI brides wave goodbye as they set off for a new life in the United States.

light that a green dray-cart filled with American soldiers and their girl-friends and drawn by two white Shire horses clattered at full speed past Hatchard's. The driver's whip was garlanded and everybody was singing 'Idaho', the melancholy strains of which were wafted away in the breeze. A notice outside St James's, Piccadilly [which had been destroyed in the Blitz] announced an open-air service in the churchyard for 6.30, and a middle-aged woman with a blue hat was putting out the chairs on the cracked flagstones between which grew the sturdy rosebay.... Two itinerant vendors were selling their wares displayed on the sandbags next to the Monseigneur – one was selling tinted spectacles, the other roses made up into buttonholes. A tall London bobby, wearing the peacetime helmet that by now had replaced the tin hat of two years earlier, was looking imperturbably at the various Military Police parading in twos round the Circus, rather like the animals that walked into the Ark – two girl soldiers with red caps and MP on their armlets, two American MPs, two French gendarmes, and a couple of Dutch *schupos*. 'Go ahead,' he seemed to say, 'you're only playing at being a policeman!'

Southeastern England was now so packed with men and materiel that the troops joked that if the invasion of northwest Europe did not come soon, England would tilt and sink beneath the weight of preparations for it. The invasion came on D-Day, 6 June 1944, carrying the war back into Hitler's 'Fortress Europe'.

FROM V-WEAPONS TO VICTORY

After the rain comes the rainbow,
You'll see the rain go,
Never fear,
We two can wait for tomorrow,
Good-bye to sorrow my dear.

On 26 May 1944 the journalist J. L. Hodson wrote in his diary: 'England is expectant, almost hushed. Every time we turn on the radio we expect to hear that the great invasion of Europe has begun.' On 6 June listeners to the Home Service heard the long-awaited announcement, read by John Snagge: 'Here is a special bulletin. . . . D-day has come. Early this morning the Allies began the assault on the northwestern face of Hitler's European fortress.'

An English housewife, Thekla Rodd, realized that it was D-Day when an accident befell her washing: 'When I am pegging out sheets on wash-day, I remember another wash-day. We knew there was something afoot, as all day and night the sky had been full of planes, wing to wing, streaming towards the coast. We did not know that it was Invasion Day. So I pegged my threadbare sheets out on the line, chatting to my neighbour meanwhile. Presently I heard her call, "The sheets! Look at the sheets!" There they hung, streaked all over with black oil, blown across from the smoke-screens. Soap was very short and the stains never did come out.'

For several days the population of England's southeast coastal areas listened to the rumble of heavy guns across the Channel, just as twenty-eight years before many of them had listened to the bombardment which had preceded the Battle of the Somme. By day and night huge convoys roared southwards to their embarkation ports.

On 12 June the Allied bridgehead in Normandy became continuous when 101 US Airborne Division captured Carentan, which commands the estuary of the Vire. This closed the last gap in the Allied front, between Omaha and Utah beaches, linking their forces together in a beach-head 42 miles wide.

On the night of the 12th the first of Hitler's 'revenge weapons', the V-1 flying bomb, chugged across the Channel. Driven by a pulse jet and guided by a gyroscopic automatic pilot, the V-1 had a speed of about 350 m.p.h., a range of 160 miles and flew at 2000–3000 feet. It could be launched from mobile catapult ramps and aircraft.

The V-1s came as a complete surprise to the British public, who at first assumed that they were downed enemy aircraft. Ten days later the Home Secretary Herbert Morrison announced that pilotless aircraft were being used against the British Isles and went on to warn, 'When the engine . . . stops and the light at the end of the machine is seen to go out, it may mean

Victory in the air. Vera Lynn relaxes with an appropriate spot of reading matter during her tour of the Far East in the autumn of 1944.

that an explosion will soon follow, perhaps in five to fifteen seconds.'

As the V-1 bombardment continued Londoners cultivated a determinedly casual attitude to this new threat. One woman recalled, 'Having lunch one day in a small restaurant in Baker St when the ominous sound of a doodle-bug [the popular nickname for the V-1] was heard and it got nearer and louder. Everyone in the restaurant gradually stopped talking and eating and froze, with knives and forks poised in mid-air until we all looked like statues. Then the usual bang was heard as a doodle-bug landed somewhere nearby, and it was wonderful to see everyone just carrying on eating and taking up their conversations without even referring to what had happened.'

Megan Ryan had a similar experience in Hampstead:

I was standing at the window, looking down at the morning scene in the street, while a buzz-bomb's sound came towards us. Across the road two women were coming out of the greengrocer's, scarves tied over their curlers, and with laden shopping-bags clutched to their stomachs they were deep in gossip. The young blind girl who walked confidently down the street twice every day on her way to and from work was rattling her stick along the kerbside barrier around the hole from which a workman was emerging, and a smartly dressed young man had crossed the road and was

Londoners turn out with gifts of food, drink and cigarettes as a long invasion convoy rolls through London on its way to the embarkation ports in June 1944.

175

about to step on to the pavement. At that moment the buzz-bomb cut out. The two women, still talking, stepped backwards into the greengrocer's; the workman slid back down the hole; the young man raised his trilby with one hand and, with the other, took the arm of the blind girl, pulling her with him into the nearest doorway. There was 'swoosh' of air, an explosion in a nearby street, and everyone moved again. The two women, still talking, came out of the shop; the workman reappeared; the blind girl inclined her head to the young man, who raised his hat, and they all continued on their way after the moment's interruption. No one had looked up or shown the slightest interest in the bomb.

The doodlebugs posed some awkward problems for the British defences, flying just a little too high for light guns and a little too low for heavier pieces, and stretching intercepting fighters to their maximum speed. To combat them, London's anti-aircraft defences were moved to the South Coast and squadrons of fighters patrolled what became known as 'flying bomb alley' above the fields of Sussex and Kent. As a long stop, an immense balloon barrage was set up on the approach to London along the 20-mile ridge between Cobham and Limpsfield. Directly beneath the barrage lay the village of Eynsford, which was the regular Sunday afternoon destination for a woman from the south London suburbs. 'There was a splendid view. . . . We could see the little hamlets nestling in the valleys . . . we could hear the larks singing . . . and we could look up and see the massive balloon barrage. If the sirens sounded, we could watch with a feeling of detachment as the "buzz bombs" roared over, seeming to thread their way between the balloons. Later on we would cycle home, often to find the house blown inside out again and fresh holes in the roof.'

The scene after a V-1 fell to earth in Clapham on 17 June, 1944. When the V-1 attacks began in that month, about 21,000 men were already at work on war-damage repair duties in the London region. By December, the number had risen to nearly 130,000. By 1945, damage repair was accounting for 40 per cent of all building work. In London the V-1s and V-2s damaged or destroyed some 600,000 houses.

Of the 9000 V-1 firings between June and September 1944, a quarter failed to cross the Channel and only a quarter tested the defences. Many collided with the balloon cables, but the great majority fell to fighters (including the British Meteor I jet fighter) and to guns firing shells fitted with the newly introduced proximity fuse. On one day only four of ninety-seven V-1s sent against London got through; two were downed by balloons, twenty-three by fighters and sixty-five by the guns. Croydon seemed to be the V-1s' favourite flight path – one vigilant dentist counted thirty-seven passing over his surgery during the course of a single day, including five in the air at the same time. Just under 6200 people were killed by the doodle-bugs and 18,000 seriously injured. In September, as their launching sites were overrun by the advancing Allies, they gave way to the V-2 rocket.

On 7 September Duncan Sandys, chairman of the government's Counter-Measures Committee, confidently told a press conference, 'Except possibly for a last few shots, the battle of London is over.' Within twenty-four hours the first V-2 had fallen on Chiswick, in London, with a tremendous detonation which was heard all over the capital. The V-2, with a range of about 215 miles, was a much more expensive weapon than the V-1, although like its predecessor it was highly inaccurate. However, it was impossible to intercept after launch, climbing as it did to 60 miles and then descending with a velocity of up to 2500 m.p.h., three to four times the speed of sound as the double 'boom' which accompanied its arrival indicated.

It was not until 10 November that Winston Churchill admitted in the House of Commons that the Germans were bombarding London with long-range rockets – during the government's long silence they had earned the ironic tag of 'flying gas mains'. In the same month Deptford was the scene of the worst V-2 disaster, when a rocket scored a direct hit on a Woolworth's crowded with Saturday-morning shoppers. One hundred and sixty died, most of them women and children.

The V-2 was preceded by no warning – if you didn't hear it you bought it. For most fortunate souls outside the blast radius there was a bright flash in the sky followed by a supersonic bang and then an ear-splitting

One of the most moving pictures of the war on the Home Front. Following a V-1 attack, a woman rescue worker lifts a distraught child from the ruins of a wrecked building in Buckingham Gate, Victoria, 23 June, 1944. The 'doodlebug' attacks were not confined to the south-east. By firing V-1s from converted bombers, the Germans spread the attacks over a wider geographical area. For example, 27 people in Oldham were killed by a V-1 on Christmas Eve, 1944. Inevitably, the V-1 onslaught prompted a fresh wave of evacuation.

Utter devastation after the fall of a V-2. The abiding memory of most people whose homes were damaged by the V-2 was the immediate aftermath of clinging dirt – from plaster, pulverised brick, dust hidden in corners and crevices and – above all – soot which was often sucked out of a chimney by the vacuum which followed the first blast wave. The historian Norman Longmate recalled the result – 'small black columns rising above the chimneys of all the houses in a road like so many exclamation marks'.

explosion. The V-2 barrage was an unnerving experience, and the art historian James Lees-Milne spoke for many Londoners when he described the threat of the rockets as 'a perpetual sword of Damocles over one's head. . . . The V-2 has become far more alarming than the V-1, quite contrary to what I thought at first, because it gives no sound. One finds oneself waiting for it, and jumping out of one's skin at the slightest bang or unexpected noise, like a car backfiring or even a door slamming.' The last of Hitler's 'revenge weapons' fell to earth on 27 March 1945, at Orpington in Kent. In all 1050 V-2s were spotted by observers, 518 of which hit London, killing 2754 people and severely injuring 6523.

Throughout 1944 small signs of peace began to nibble away at the panoply of wartime restrictions and regulations. In February the Board of Trade relaxed the regulation which, with the aim of saving textiles, had prohibited turn-ups on men's trousers, limited the number of pockets on their jackets and snipped 2 inches off their shirt tails. Hugh Dalton, President of the Board of the Trade, explained the removal of the restrictions with the memorable comment, 'On the whole we have done something to lift the morale of the country – particularly the morale of the men. The morale of the women has always been high, but that of the men has been depressed by not having enough pockets.'

In September Civil Defence outside the London area was virtually disbanded, and on the 17th of that month the blackout gave way to a 'dim-out', although it remained in force in all coastal areas and for a distance of 5 miles inland, and was briefly reimposed during the V-2 campaign.

When people removed their blackout material there were some nasty surprises. A civil servant from the Devon village of Branscombe discovered that taking down the blackout was an extremely messy business as the dust and dead insects which had accumulated behind the shutters for five years now descended on him in an avalanche. After the rigours of 'make do and mend', economy often took precedence over elation at the disappearance of an unwelcome restriction. A Birmingham woman recalled, 'We did not go mad and burn the materials. They came in handy for years.'

On Christmas Day 1944 churches were allowed to light their stained-glass windows, and a few days later car headlight masks were abolished. As the end of the war approached, many pre-war activities made a welcome return: you could buy a large-scale map, use a car radio, sleep in an uncamouflaged tent, and even release racing pigeons without police permission. However, it was not until after the war had ended that 'spreading alarm and despondency' ceased to be a punishable offence.

There had been some alarm during the V-weapon campaign and much despondency throughout the bitterly cold winter of 1944–45, with its seemingly endless queues and fuel shortages. A December entry in the diary of a London housewife captures the glum mood of the last winter of the war: 'Absolutely nothing of note this week; fog, which has made me lose my way coming home . . . ice and frost . . . the usual accompaniment of bangs from rockets . . . sirens one evening early and two doodles

A famous cricketing picture. A doodlebug stops play at Lords on 29 July, 1944 during a game between the Army and the RAF. Assuming the prone position are batsman Jack Robertson of the Army XI, wicketkeeper Andy Wilson of the RAF XI and Squadron Leader Bill Edrich at slip. When play resumed, Robertson hit a six off the first ball.

VE-Day has arrived and excited revellers take a truck ride through central London on their way to hear the keynote speech of the day, delivered by Winston Churchill.

droning over the house . . . a hateful boil on my neck. . . . People in the office have colds, pains and aches in limbs and crawl about with overcoats on and shawls draped about them. . . . With only cardboard and mica windows and no doors or walls to keep out the draughts it is pretty freezing and it seems our legs will never be felt again.'

Hopes of a speedy victory in Europe had risen in September 1944 as Allied forces raced through the Low Countries. They had been dashed in December by Hitler's last great offensive, in the Ardennes, but by the following March it was clear that Germany was on the verge of collapse.

In April there was a rush to buy flags and bunting for the victory celebrations. In London the counters of the West End stores suddenly sprouted small forests of patriotic flags and streamers. Business was brisk, and by common consent Selfridge's flag department was the best stocked and its displays the most imaginative. Large and small Union Jacks took pride of place alongside flags of the colonies and banners bearing portraits of George VI and the legend 'God Save the King'. Another popular item was a 'Welcome Home' flag for returning prisoners-of-war. The Selfridge's buyer confided, 'We've been busy for the last two to three weeks, but we haven't got to the same pitch as we did last September when Paris fell. We did amazing business then – people simply thought the war was going to end by October. But business is warming up. . . . The average person pays 25s to 30s for a flag and we do a considerable trade in streamers at 7s 3d.'

But when was the war going to end? For at least a week before it became a fact the announcement of peace was expected almost hourly. The rush of events was reflected in the headlines of the *Daily Express*:

Tuesday, 1 May: 'Nazi Radio "Goodbye"'
Wednesday, 2 May: 'Hitler is Dead'
Thursday, 3 May: 'Army of 100,000 Surrenders'
Friday 4 May: 'British Enter Denmark'
Saturday, 5 May: 'Germans Surrender inside Monty's Tent'
Monday, 7 May: 'The Last Hours'

'The Last Hours' was a suitably vague headline, fashioned to cover the uncertainty which hung over the closing moments of the war. Rumours abounded, and there was a pricking feeling of anti-climax. As a Londoner told Mass-Observation, 'What strikes me is that the war's ending in just the same phoney way as it began. "It's peace. It isn't peace. They've surrendered. They haven't surrendered." It does bring back those first months when there was and there wasn't a war.'

On 7 May anticipation mounted. That afternoon in London a big crowd gathered outside the railings of Buckingham Palace, scanning the windows for the slightest sign of movement and watching workmen laying a carpet and erecting a platform on the balcony from which the King and Queen were to appear. At about 6.30 p.m. one of the workmen at the Palace gate gave a shrug of his shoulders, a gesture of disappointment which communicated itself to the crowd. He and his mates climbed down their ladders, from which they had been fixing loudspeakers. Slowly the crowd began to melt away, leaving behind two young girls in paper hats perched defiantly on the Victoria Memorial opposite.

Outside London the early evening passed quietly. A Chepstow woman visiting Bristol wrote in her diary: 'The same crowds were bustling home from work, as it is now 5 p.m., and stood patiently in queues looking as if their only aim in life at the moment is to get home as quickly as possible after a day's toil.' A young woman who had served as an air-raid warden in the Midlands went to a wardens' party at her local pub: 'The pub was as quiet as a church – at least for about the first hour. We sat around drinking mild on a very modest scale, exchanged reminiscences about the Blitz, deplored the Polish deadlock, refused to buy some very shoddy red, white and blue favours which were being hawked around. . . . People were singing the songs of the last war, but in a rather laboured and not very spontaneous way.'

At last, at about 7.40 p.m., the Ministry of Information put the nation out of its misery, issuing a statement on the radio. In a curious way it fell almost as flat as Neville Chamberlain's gloomy declaration of war on 3 September 1939: 'It is understood that, in accordance with arrangements between the three great powers, an official announcement will be broadcast by the Prime Minister at three o'clock tomorrow, Tuesday afternoon, 8 May. In view of this fact, tomorrow, Tuesday, will be treated as Victory-in-Europe Day and will be regarded as a holiday. His Majesty the King will broadcast to the people of the British Empire and Commonwealth tomorrow, Tuesday, at 9 p.m.' Thus, in the fussy, precise tones of a civil servant, was VE Day brought to the British public.

As midnight approached a young housewife went up to the roof of her flat in London's Edgware Road '. . . from which my husband and I have so often watched fires flaring up in a ring around London as far as we could see, and seen explosions, listened to bombs and planes and guns during the "Little Blitz" of spring '44; also watched buzz bombs with their flaring tails careering along over the houses before the final "bang". . . . As I looked, fireworks began to erupt around the horizon and the red glow of distant bonfires lit the sky – peaceful and joyous fires now, in place of the terrifying ones of the last years.'

As midnight struck, the big ships riding at anchor in ports from the

Perched above a huge crowd in Piccadilly Circus, a small band of intrepid urban mountaineers celebrate on the statueless, boarded-up plinth of Eros.

Firth of Clyde to Southampton opened up their sirens in deep-throated, booming V-signals. Smaller craft followed them with a cacophony of hoots and whistles and searchlights flashed out a V in Morse across the sky. The noise could be heard for miles inland, and people living on the coast, thrilled by the din, defied the continuing blackout regulations, threw open their curtains and let their lights blaze out into the night.

In London there was a violent thunderstorm, reminding Londoners of the great storm which had burst over the capital on the last night of peace, 2 September 1939, and also providing an echo of the Blitz.

The mood on the morning of VE-Day was quiet and reflective. For many housewives the reflecting was done in yet more queues. In the Surrey town of Dorking one of the Mass-Observation team noted: '8.30 a.m. – crowds lined up at the bakeries, the first time I had seen this since the New Year Fire Blitz. There is not nearly enough bread to go round.' A London woman wrote in her diary: 'May 8, Tuesday, a thunderstorm greeted VE-Day, but was over before I went to join the longest fish queue I can remember.'

For several hours the mood remained subdued, as people adjusted to the notion of peace. The writer and editor John Lehmann recalled:

> My chief recollection of VE-Day is of queuing for a bus to Paddington that never came, and finally having to walk across Hyde Park with a heavy suitcase in one hand and a briefcase in the other, pouring with sweat. The crowds were more dazed than excited, and they seemed to gather more and more, in a slow groundswell, no wild battering of waves, good-tempered, a little bewildered and awkward about celebrating, like cripples taking the first steps after a miraculous healing, not fully grasping yet the implications of the new life ahead of them. Now the noise of the last all-clear on the sirens seemed to prolong itself in the mind's ear until it was beyond the range of hearing for ever.

In the early afternoon things began to pick up. Emerging from the Beefsteak Club and strolling down Parliament Square, Harold Nicolson noted:

> I find the streets very crowded and people wearing all manner of foolish paper caps and cheering slightly. When I leave the club at 2.15, I find the roads packed. Trafalgar Square is a seething mass of people with figures draped over the lions. Whitehall is overflowing, but a few buses tried to push their way through. After the Cenotaph it is just a jam. I squeeze in behind a car and manage to reach the House at about five to three. I pause to recover myself in Palace Yard and regret to observe that I have torn a hole in my new suit.

At 3 p.m. came Churchill's speech from Downing Street, relayed by loudspeaker to the crowds in Parliament Square and beyond them across the nation. The thousands in Parliament Square listened intently, raising a great cheer when the Prime Minister announced that from midnight hostilities were to cease, and another to greet the news that 'our dear Channel Islands [occupied by German forces since June 1940] were to be liberated. There was a flurry of flag-waving when the Prime Minister came to the point in his speech at which he declared, 'The German war is therefore at an end.' As he finished, the buglers of the Royal Horse Guards sounded the Cease Fire. Then, as the plangent notes faded away on the balmy afternoon air, the band struck up 'God Save the King'. Soldiers and civilians stood to attention and sang the National Anthem with a fervour which reminded one observer of the 'singing of a sacred hymn'.

This was the moment for Churchill to bask in the glow of victory. Huge crowds followed his car as it inched its way from Downing Street to the House of Commons. Later, as he walked back from a service of thanksgiving at St Margaret's Church, Westminster, he was engulfed again. People ran or stood on tiptoe to see him, or held up their babies so that years hence they could be told that they had seen the Great Man on the Great Day. From all sides the cry went up, 'Winnie, Winnie!' One battered old Cockney woman, clearly happily drunk, bawled out, 'That's 'im, that's 'is little old lovely bald head!' As Churchill re-entered the Houses of Parliament, a small boy (Master Peter Bland of Golders Green), who had been pursuing the Prime Minister all the way back from St Margaret's Church, finally caught up with him on the threshold of the Members' Lobby and asked him for his autograph. He was not to be denied with gruff refusals. Churchill solemnly took off his glasses, ruffled the lad's hair and signed his book, observing, 'That will remind you of a glorious day.'

This was only the beginning of Churchill's day. At 4 p.m. he drove to Buckingham Palace, brandishing his trademark, a big cigar. A huge crowd cheered wildly as he appeared with the Royal Family on the balcony at the Palace. The King was bare-headed and wearing a naval uniform; Her Majesty was dressed in blue, as was the fourteen-year-old Princess Margaret; Princess Elizabeth appeared in her uniform of a second subaltern of the ATS.

An hour later Churchill was addressing another massive crowd which had gathered below the windows of the Ministry of Health building in Whitehall. As he gave the V-sign, the crowd roared itself hoarse. Then he addressed the crowd: 'This is your victory. It is the victory of the cause of freedom in every land. In all our long history we have never seen a greater day than this. Everyone, man or woman, has done their best. Everyone has tried. Neither the long years, nor the dangers, nor the fierce attacks of the enemy have in any way weakened the deep resolve of the British nation. God bless you all.'

At 9 p.m. a less naturally gifted orator made the second keynote speech of the day. It was one of the King's longest broadcasts, lasting thirteen minutes, and the millions who listened had his painful stammer uppermost in their minds, a handicap which increased the affection in which he was held by the nation. As one listener commented: 'At 9 p.m. the King. Most people that I know seem to feel the same about his speeches. Admiration for the way he faces his difficulties, fear that he shall trip up, and a kind of personal embarrassment when he seems likely to do so. I'm afraid it rather distracts from his matter sometimes, but it can't be helped and, anyway, it gives an impression of common humanity which no oratory can do.'

A popular song of 1943 had anticipated the end of the war:

> *I'm going to get lit up when the lights go up*
> * in London,*
> *I'm going to get lit up as I've never been*
> * before;*
> *You will find me on the tiles, you will find me*
> * wreathed in smiles;*
> *I'm going to get lit up so I'll be visible for*
> * miles.*

Victory searchlights blaze into the sky above St Paul's Cathedral. On VE-Day many small children, accustomed to the black-out, were alarmed by the illuminations.

All dressed up and nowhere to go. The people of Leeds drag a reluctant Hitler towards the bonfire which awaits him.

As darkness fell, the milling crowds in London were able to savour the unfamiliar brightness of the floodlighting of public buildings and the illumination of cinemas and theatres. Among the more extrovert, inhibitions fell away. The MP Tom Driberg was watching the scene in central London.

> In the orange glow that streamed down from the Tivoli to the pavement of the Strand, a buxom woman in an apron made of a Union Jack and a man of respectable middle-class appearance did an exaggeratedly Latin-American dance while an accordion played 'South of the Border'. . . . As I picked my unobtrusive way along Coventry Street, a cheerful woman bawled, 'MPs – yer off duty tonight!' I started guiltily; but she was addressing two Redcaps [military policemen]. On the roof above Scott's dignified oyster house an airman and a Yank did a fantastic Harold Lloyd act, elaborately sharing a bottle, tossing coins down to the people, who screamed each time they swayed over the parapet.

In London and across the nation, the night sky was lit by thousands of bonfires, at the top of which were perched effigies of Hitler and his henchmen. A correspondent in the *Hereford Times* wrote a vivid account of the bonfire in the small village of Stoke Lacy:

Passing through the village of Stoke Lacy early on Tuesday afternoon one was startled to see an effigy of Hitler in the car park at the Plough. That evening a crowd began to gather, and word went around that Hitler was to be consumed in flames at 11 p.m. At that hour excitement was intense, when Mr W. R. Symonds called upon Mr S. J. Parker, the Commander of No. 12 Platoon of the Home Guard, to set the effigy alight. In a few minutes the body of Hitler disintegrated as his 1000 years' empire had done. First his arm, poised in the Hitler salute, dropped as smartly as it was ever raised in life. . . . Then a leg fell off, and the flames burnt fiercely to the strains of 'Rule Britannia', 'There'll Always Be an England' and 'Roll out the Barrel'. Then the crowd spontaneously linked hands and in a circle 300 strong sang 'Auld Lang Syne'. Mr Parker then called for three cheers for Mr Churchill, President Truman, Marshal Stalin and our serving boys and girls. The ceremony was followed by the singing of 'God Save the King'.

The bonfires often involved elaborate preparations, and the events of the day – street parties, sports meetings and fancy-dress parades – were organized around them. In Hanover Road, in north London, the community's young people had made their own posters and set them up at each end of the street. Small children were instructed to bring as many of their friends as they could, while the older boys made their own fireworks (a rather alarming proposition). Everybody had a hand in making the Hitler effigy. One lady provided the jacket, another the trousers and so on until the Führer's uniform was as authentic as possible. A dressmaker living in the road gave him the finishing touches. The Chief Fire Watcher in Hanover Road made the face, the boys fitted up the gallows from which he was hanged, and the adults laid the foundations of the bonfire. Then someone suggested that they burn Goering too, and soon the fat Reichsmarshal – complete with rows of Iron Crosses – was seated on a chair at Hitler's feet. Next to them was a battered doll, face and body darkened with red paint as a reminder of the misery the Nazis had brought to humanity. The bonfire was lit at 9.30 p.m., and almost immediately Adolf began to go up in flames. Amid cries of 'Don't let him end up so soon, let him linger', a hose was turned on the effigy in order to prolong the burning.

Union Jacks are waved as bonfire flames leap into the night. Amid the celebrations, the lights and fires reminded many people of the dark days of the Blitz.

The poignant addition of the mutilated doll to the Hanover Road bonfire was an apt symbol of the heartache and suffering of the war years. The crackling fires spoke of victory and release from fear, but they could not banish all the shadows of the recent past. The novelist William Sansom had spent the war as an auxiliary fireman and had played a leading role in the documentary *Fires Were Started*, Humphrey Jennings's moving tribute to the Auxiliary Fire Service. Watching the fires reflected in the London sky, his thoughts turned back to the Blitz:

> Pinpointed across the City [of Westminster] appeared the first urgent firebursts, ever growing, as though they were in fact spreading, as each bonfire reddened and cast its coppery glow on the house-rows, on glassy windows and the black blind spaces where windows had once been. Alleys lit up, streets took on the fireset glare – it seemed that in each dark declivity of houses there lurked the old fire. The ghosts of wardens and fireguards and firemen were felt scurrying again down in the redness. Fireworks peppered the air with a parody of gunfire. The smell of burning wood charred the nostrils. And, gruesomely correct, some of the new street lights and fluorescent window lights . . . glowed fiercely blueish-white, bringing again the shrill memory of the old white thermite glare of the bursting incendiary.

VJ-Day, marking the end of the war against Japan, was celebrated on 16 August. In his diary a Liverpool businessman noted that in Kirby

> there were no signs of joy, of enthusiasm, no cheering crowds, all shops shut and the streets almost deserted. Maybe most of us are mentally and physically exhausted; maybe we have become so accustomed to living under war-time restraints we have not yet realized that the fighting has stopped. I can only speak for myself on this day. I feel no elation, no uplifting of the spirit, only a sort of dumb inarticulate thankfulness that the hell of war, the killing, the misery is over. . . .
>
> At night we went to Caldy Hill to see the bonfires blazing on the distant Welsh hills. What pleased us more was to see the opposite side of the Dee twinkling with thousands of street lamps and lighted windows. So we went

home, opened wide the curtains and switched on every light in the house. More than anything else did this action, one taken by nearly everyone, bring home to us the fact that the war has ended.

The war had been won but the cupboard was almost bare. At the time of VJ-Day a Somerset housewife reflected, 'In spite of the joy one can't help reflecting that our larders are bare, there are no houses for our returning soldiers. . . . Everyone's house needs painting and replastering, our clothes are shabby, and one can't buy a sheet or a blanket unless one is bombed-out or a newly-wed. . . . Life is going to be every bit as strenuous; we are all exhausted. . . . The best minute of the day has been just to sit down and realize that the war is over.'

The cinema and theatre lights which had dazzled the crowds on VE-Day had been snapped off again to save fuel. There was less meat in the shops than there had been a year before. In May the bacon ration had been reduced, and in September the clothing ration was reduced to 36 coupons a year. In 1946 bread was rationed.

Fighting and winning the war had saddled Britain with colossal overseas debts, and she was now facing a 'financial Dunkirk'. At home as many as 4 million homes, almost a third of the total stock, had been damaged by enemy action, including half a million totally destroyed. The housing shortage was to be one of the major preoccupations of the Labour government which was elected in July 1945.

On the credit side of the balance sheet was the modernization and reinvigoration of Britain's farming industry, a development fore-shadowed in the 1930s and accelerated by wartime planning. Between 1938 and 1944 the total area of tilled land increased by 5 million acres and the total net output of calories was doubled. Yields were boosted by the increased use of fertilizers, the quadrupling of the number of tractors employed on farms, and a far-reaching system of loans and subsidies. The war also acted as a powerful stimulus to industries which were to be vital to Britain's economic survival in the postwar years – motor vehicles, electronics, aircraft and chemicals; high-technology developments in radar, nuclear power, jet propulsion and antibiotics carved out an important role for science in British industry.

In spite of the severities and sacrifices on the Home Front, the war brought many gains for working-class people and their families. There was full employment, wages kept well ahead of prices, and rationing, with its guarantee that essential fuels and goods reached everyone, ensured that for millions of people life was better throughout the war than it had been in the 1930s.

Finally, the measures taken to fight a total war in themselves had a long-lasting effect on postwar social policy. Few will deny that we are not better off for the National Health Service, whose origins lay in the national Emergency Hospital Scheme established in 1939. For all this a human price had been paid. On 8 May 1945 the twenty-six-year-old Meg Ryan reflected on the six years of war:

When they began I'd been twenty, full of the enthusiasm, ambitions, certainties and energies of youth. I'd married and borne children, but the war had stolen from us the simple ordinary joys of a young couple shaping a shared life. Our first home had been burnt to rubble and with it had gone many of the gifts which relatives and friends had given us and which should have been treasured for life, while what had been salvaged would always bear the marks of that night of destruction. We had known the agony of separation and the too rare, too short, too heightened joys of reunions.

Demobilisation. An ex-serviceman tries on his 'demob' clothes. By the end of 1945 about 30,000 demobbed men a week were turning to the Resettlement Advice Service for help in their return to civilian life.

Apart, we had endured illnesses and dangers and fears for each other. As a family too we had been separated and now must learn to live together, overcoming the barriers set up by experiences which had not been shared. . . .

I thought of those who had been dear to us who had not lived to see this. . . . Of John, who had stood at the altar with us on our wedding day, John, who had . . . been trapped in his cockpit when his plane sank beneath the waves. . . . Of Ron, constant companion of my brother since schooldays . . . who had vanished without trace when the troopship he was on had been sunk by the Japanese; of Peter, my girlhood friend's gay, kind brother . . . who had been shot while trying to escape from the prisoner-of-war camp to which he'd been taken. . . . They were all so young. The youngest died at nineteen the oldest at twenty-four. I sat thinking of them . . . and then went indoors to stand looking at the sleeping faces of my two little sons, whose lives lay before them in a world of peace.

One of the first 'prefabricated' homes to be built in Britain, in January 1945. Conceived as a temporary solution to the housing shortage, the 'prefab' became a permanent feature of the postwar urban landscape.

ACKNOWLEDGEMENTS

Grateful acknowledgement is made to the publishers and copyright holders for permission to reproduce previously published material from the following:

Books
The authors are especially indebted to *The Home Front* edited by Norman Longmate (Chatto & Windus, 1981) as a source of both factual information and quotations.
Living Through the Blitz by Tom Harrisson, Collins 1976
Material from the Mass-Observation Archive © The Tom Harrisson Mass-Observation Archive, University of Sussex. Reprinted by permission of Curtis Brown Ltd.
London's Burning by Constantine Fitzgibbon, Macdonald 1970
The Lessons of London by Ritchie Calder, Secker & Warburg 1941
Raiders Overhead by Barbara Nixon, Scolar Press 1980
The Homeguard of Britain by Charles Graves, Hutchinson 1943
Postscripts by J. B. Priestley, reprinted by permission of William Heinemann Ltd
Mrs Milburn's Diaries: An Englishwoman's Day to Day Reflections 1939–45, Harrap 1979
The Evacuees by B. S. Johnson, Gollancz 1965
The Sheltered Days by Derek Lambert, Andre Deutsch 1965
'Swing-Song' by Louis MacNeice reprinted by permission of Faber & Faber Ltd from *The Collected Poems of Louis Macneice*
A Pullet in the Midden by Rachel Knappett, Michael Joseph 1947
Bureaucrats in Battledress by Henry Smith, R. E. Jones, Conway 1945
Kentish Fire by Hubert S. Banner, Hurst & Blackett 1944
Unconditional Surrender by Evelyn Waugh, Penguin 1981
If Only Their Mothers Knew by Shirley Joseph, Faber & Faber 1946
I Am My Brother by John Lehmann, Longman 1960
Diaries and Letters 1930–64, Harold Nicolson, Collins 1980
Westminster At War by William Samson, Faber & Faber 1947
A Job at the BBC by Joseph MacLeod, William McLellan, Glasgow 1947
One Man in His Time by Bruce Belfrage, Hodder & Stoughton 1951
School Errant by J. M. Leakey, Dulwich College Preparatory School, 1951
Red Roses Every Night
Joan Wildish's Diary quoted in *The Guardian*, 11 February 1989. Manuscript: Imperial War Museum
I.T.M.A. 1939–48 by Francis Worsley, Vox Mundi 1948

Songs
We'll Meet Again by Parker, Charles. Copyright © 1939 by Dash Music Co. Ltd, 8/9 Frith Street, London W1. Reproduced by permission. All rights reserved.
I'm Going to Get Lit Up by H. Gregg © 1943. Reproduced by permission of Peter Maurice Music Co. Ltd, London
The Washing on the Siegfried Line by M. Carr, J. Kennedy © 1939. Reproduced by permission of Peter Maurice Music Co. Ltd, London
She's the Girl That Makes the Thing Reproduced by permission of the Trustees of the Mass-Observation Archive, University of Sussex
Over There, Cohan. Warner Chappell Music Ltd
Hey, Little Hen Words and music by Ralph Butler and Noel Gay. Published by Noel Gay Music Company Ltd

BBC Broadcast
As broadcast by L. D. MacGregor on the BBC Home Service, 18 April 1941

Picture Acknowledgements
ZEC *Daily Mirror* London 123T; Michael Head **IV**; Hulton Picture Company 6, 9, 11, 13, 14BR, 14BL, 15T, 15B, 16T, 18, 20B, 21TR, 22, 28B, 29TL, 41, 73B, 81T,B, 85, 94, 106, 119T, 131, 147B,L, 159, 168, 170T,B 171T, 172, Imperial War Museum **XII, XIX, XX, XXII, XXIII, XXIV,** 8, 14T, 21TL, 29TR,B, 31BR, **32,** 35, 37, 47T, 53, 54–5, 61, 62B, 67, 68, 71T,B, 75T,B, 77, 78, 81BL, 83, 84T,C, 90, 95, 97, 100, 103BR,T, 104, 105, 107, 112B, 113, 115, 122, 123, 125, 135, 136, 140, 151, 154, 156, 157, 164, 166, 171BR,BL, 181, 183, 185, 186; Imperial War Museum/Robert Opie Collection/Photo Angelo Hornak **XXV**; Kobal Collection 142BL, 143, 146B, 147TL,TR,BR; London Express News & Features 126B; Vera Lynn Collection **4, 7,** 19T, 51, 65, 117, 127, 129, 133, 141, 142, 150, 155, 165, 174; Mander & Mitchenson Theatre Collection **137, 138;** Marylebone Cricket Club 179; National Film Archive 146T; National Museum of Photography/*Daily Herald* Collection 180, 184, 187T; Robert Opie Collection **I, II, III, V, VI, VII, VIII, IX, XV, XVI, XVIII;** Popperfoto Title page, 2, 12, 16B, 17, 20T, 23T,B, 28TL, 30B, 31BL, 33, 34, 36, 38, 39, 42T,B, 46T,B, **47B,** 48T,B, 49, 59, 63, 70, 71B, 73T, 74, 84B,C, 88, 89, 91, 96, 99, 101, 110, 111, 114T,B, 116T,B, 117B, **120,** 129, 124T,B, 153, 162R,TL, 163TL,TR,B, 167, 173, 175, 176, 177, 178; Popperfoto/Esten **X, XI;** Popperfoto/Jame Jarché **XXI,** 119B; Popperfoto/Saidman **XIII, XIV, XVII;** Punch 82T,B, 148; Sport and General Press Agency 29CR; John Topham Picture Library 30T, 62T, 102T,BL, 103BL, 112T, 139, 187B, 188, 189